Triumph on the Gallows

FIRST EDITION — March 1950
SECOND EDITION — May 1950
THIRD EDITION — September 1950

TRIUMPH
on the
GALLOWS

By
ITZHAK GURION

Published by
American Memorial Committee
for the
HANGED MARTYRS OF ERETZ ISRAEL
602 Troy Avenue, Brooklyn, N. Y.
and
BRIT TRUMPELDOR OF AMERICA
5711 - 1950

Third Edition

Printed by Futuro Press, Inc.
476 Broadway, New York.
 200

To the officers and soldiers of the Irgun who, through their heroism and sacrifices, made possible the liberation of Israel.

To those Americans who recall with pride this country's fight for independence and therefore lent their sympathetic support to the fighters for the independence of Eretz Israel.

To my beloved wife, Zipora, who more than once saw her husband and children carried off to prison in the middle of the night by British troops, and on the morrow carried on in our absence.

To my children who in the tender years of their lives experienced "Bevin's University"—British prisons and concentration camps

This book is dedicated.

Prologue

NO one but Itzhak Gurion could have written this book. It took the sensitivity of a poet to describe the martyrdom of those who died so heroically to wrest back the ancient land of Israel from the unclean hands that have held it. Here are the images of these men and the fortitude of their souls. Here also is the picture of the henchmen and the weak-kneed lackeys of the British Government and the whole sordid business of holding a people in thraldom.

In fluent language that seems almost effortless, Gurion describes the last days of his fighting comrades in the death cells of British prisons in Israel, and I, for one, shall never again hear the HATIKVAH without thinking of the men who sang it on the way to the gallows—on which they died to make Israel live.

Here is irrefutable proof that the land of Israel would still be a dependence of its former usurpers were it not for the farsightedness and the heroism of those who realized that it could be won back by force, force of character and blood. Two thousand years of cruel oppression died at the end of the rope on which dangled the bodies of Dov Gruner and his fighting friends. If anyone can read Mr. Gurion's book without feeling proud of belonging to the people he describes let him remove himself as far as he can from them; let him never again say that he is of the same ancestry.

KONRAD BERCOVICI

CONTENTS

Cover illustration by Arthur Szyk.

Foreword

THE achievements of the Jewish Underground in Palestine will never be forgotten either by the Jewish people or the world at large. But the men who heroically sacrificed their lives to make these exploits possible are all too quickly being forgotten.

The men of the Jewish Underground were not ordinary soldiers in a regular army. Nor were they typical of the fighters of other national revolutions. Not only the might of a great empire, but all the malignance which lives in the twisted soul of the ghetto was directed toward crushing them. The land in which they fought was little larger than the State of New Jersey. It was occupied by no less than 100,000 British troops and inhabited by many more Arabs than Jews. The Jewish fighters were faced with the active opposition of the leaders of the Zionist Movement and the so-called "official" leadership of the Palestine

Jewish community. They were hounded and hunted not only by the British and their Arab spies, but also by Jewish collaborators. Their's was not merely a military uprising but a revolution against the terrible effects which two thousand years of abnormal life had produced in the Jews.

Here then is the story of these men, told by one who was not only their friend but also their comrade-in-arms.

It is a tale which contains elements of the rebellious poetry of Bialik, the joyful music of David, the proud, undefeated tears of Israel itself.

Brit Trumpeldor of America

Preface to Second and Third Editions

THE enthusiastic reception accorded the first edition of "Triumph on the Gallows"; the many appreciative letters received by the Memorial Committee and the author; the warm, appreciative comments it has received in the press; and particularly the speed with which the first edition was sold convinced the publisher of the necessity of issuing a second and then a third edition.

The success thus achieved by "Triumph on the Gallows," I ascribe entirely to the good will and high esteem which Americans held and continue to hold for the *Irgun* and all it stood for.

Americans have a great share in the victory of the *Irgun*. The record of that triumph represents a part of the heritage not only of Israel but of America as well.

The American Memorial Committee for the Hanged Martyrs of Eretz Israel, which aims to establish in Israel a fitting living memorial to the martyred hanged heroes, has undertaken to discharge some responsibility for that heritage. It undertook the publication of "Triumph on the Gallows" in order that the entire net proceeds, together with all contributions it receives shall be dedicated to that worthy purpose. I am certain that all freedom loving Americans will give the Committee their support and encouragement.

To all those who took their time to write me and offer valuable advice and suggestion, I am deeply thankful.

To Messrs. Samuel Bookspan, Israel Baratz and Elazar Ben Aaron, who were largely responsible for bringing the Committee into being and whose valuable assistance made possible the presentation of "Triumph on the Gallows" to the American public, I offer thanks in my own name and in behalf of those to whom this book is respectfully dedicated.

I. G.

Rosh Hashana 5711—*Sept.* 1950

Preface

SOON after the publication in the Yiddish press of sections of this book, *Brit Trumpeldor of America* proposed that it be made available to the American public in its entirety in English translation.

The suggestion appealed to me for many reasons. The American reader ought to come to know those heroic spirits who went to the gallows with supreme fortitude and with the conviction of the champion of freedom, who gives his life for an oppressed people and knows that his hanging constitutes in reality a blow struck against the tyrannical conqueror.

Americans followed with bated breath the development of the Jewish revolt in Palestine during 1944-48. The struggle for Jewish liberation vividly recalled to the American people its own war of independence. There are striking similarities between the two struggles for freedom. The oppressor was the same. British colonial brutalization, hangings and the denial of basic human rights typified both the American and Jewish revolts. The American people saw in the fighters of the Jewish Underground the twentieth-century counterparts of George Washington and Tom Paine. It drew a parallel between Dov

13

Gruner and Nathan Hale, both of whom were captured by the British, tried before "military courts" and hanged because they dared take up arms to free their countries.

Before his execution, Nathan Hale said: "*I only regret that I have but one life to give for my country.*" Dov Gruner's last words were: "*What pains me now with the end so near is the awareness that I have not done enough for my country.*"

The men of the Jewish Underground and its commanders received inspiration and assurance of victory from the heroes of the American Revolution. Instead of making a statement in his own behalf, one of the soldiers of the *Irgun Zvai Leumi* (The National Military Organization) on trial for his life before a British "military court" felt moved to read aloud . . . the American Declaration of Independence of July 4th, 1776.

How applicable were those words:

> "When in the course of human events, it becomes necessary for one people to dissolve the political bonds which have connected them with another, and to assume among the powers of the earth, the separate and equal station to which the Laws of Nature and of Nature's God entitle them, a decent respect to the opinions of mankind requires that they should declare the causes which impel them to the separation.
>
> "We hold these truths to be self-evident, that all men are created equal, that they are endowed by their Creator with certain inalienable rights . . . that whenever any form of government becomes destructive of these ends, it is the right of the people to alter it or abolish it . . . when a long train of abuses and usurpations, pursuing invariably the same object, evidence a design to reduce them under absolute despotism, it is their right, it is their duty, to throw off such government. . . ."

When the thirteen colonies began their revolt against British oppression, there were some, called Tories, who had no stomach for freedom or independence. They were satisfied with colonial status under the British crown, and regarded Washington and his followers as a band of unhinged fanatics.

It is easy to imagine what the result would have been had the Tories and not the minutemen prevailed. The colonies would have remained typical British possessions, poor, neglected and exploited. How fortunate for the world, England and America that the Tories did not have their way.

It is understandable, therefore, why the freedom loving people of America backed the Jewish Underground in its struggle for the liberation of Israel.

Menachem Beigin, leader of the Jewish Freedom Movement in Israel, was certainly right when, on his recent visit to the United States, he stated in one of his speeches, that the fighters for freedom throughout the world were members of one family, despite differences in religion and nationality.

Yet, if there are many parallels between the revolts of the American and Jewish peoples, there are basic differences as regards the early development of the two countries. In the United States, those who drove out the British constituted the first government and infused their passion for liberty into the fabric of the new nation. The American teacher proudly tells his pupils of the noble death of Nathan Hale. His valor is recorded in American history books and on the monument which the City of New York erected in honor of its hero. The Commander of America's Revolutionary Army was this nation's first and most beloved President.

The inner political development of the State of Israel, however, has followed an entirely different course. At the head of the Provisional Government there stood, after the successful revolt, a group of men who had either opposed or, at best, had not participated in the struggle against the British. Some had even collaborated with the oppressor against the Underground forces. Hence the readiness to yield the legitimate Jewish rights to the historic boundaries of the Land of Israel. Hence also the attempt to minimize the importance of the revolt and the honor due its participants.

* * *

In this book, I have attempted to present to the reader only a few chapters in the recent Jewish rebellion. The chief characters are those young men who made the supreme sacrifice for Israel's freedom by dying heroically on the gallows of the British enemy.

When, in 1944, Menachem Beigin proclaimed the revolt, the Irgun Zvai Leumi numbered but four hundred poorly trained and badly equipped fighters. In the course of the four year struggle, thousands joined up and the operations of the Jewish Underground increased in scope and military effectiveness, attracting the attention of the entire world.

The geography of Eretz Israel is not suited to underground warfare. It is an extremely small country without great forests or satisfactory mountain ranges where groups of guerilla fighters and armories may be hidden. The Irgun was, by and large, restricted to the towns and a few villages. Yet neither the British Army nor the huge British police establishment could prevail against the Jewish underground. On the contrary, the British were compelled to seek safety in self imposed "Ghettos"—called fortresses. They did not find safety, however, even within their "Ghettos." The British forces in Eretz Israel were paralized by the unrelenting blows of the Underground, and were compelled to leave the country.

The complete story of the Irgun's fight is still not public knowledge. The soldiers and officers of the Underground were familiar, only with those aspects of the struggle with which they were themselves concerned. Only the Commander-in-Chief, Menachem Beigin, who coordinated all activities, knows the whole story. Even those who were close to the Irgun's dramatic development are eagerly awaiting the publication of Mr. Beigin's account of the struggle, at present still being written.

I was in charge of the Irgun section which was responsible for the welfare of Irgun soldiers captured by the British. I was also liaison officer with the official Jewish community and municipal institutions, and with the attorneys who defended our captured soldiers.

It was in this capacity that I observed, at close hand, the events leading up to the execution of our fighters, and it is only this phase of the dramatic rebellion that I will deal with in the pages following.

*   *   *

It is altogether fitting that the American branch of *Brit Trumpeldor (Betar)* should undertake the publication of this volume. *Betar* educated the generation of Jewish fighters which made possible the reconstitution of the State of Israel. From out of the ranks of *Betar,* came the majority of the soldiers and leaders of the Jewish Underground Armies. The history of the Jewish revolt mirrors the struggle of *Betar,* its strivings, pain and suffering. The Jewish patriots who died on the British gallows in Palestine drew their strength and spirit of sacrifice from the teachings of Zeev Jabotinsky, *Rosh Betar* (Head of Betar). Shlomo Ben Yosef and Dov Gruner were *Betarim.* The Commander of the Irgun, Menachem Beigin, was a leader of *Betar.* The anthem of the *Irgun* was the hymn of *Betar,* and the breath of life of the *Irgun* was the spirit of *Betar.*

Group of Betarim, upon graduation from "Hachshara," preparing to leave for
Eretz-Israel. Shlomo Ben Yosef is fourth from left in second row.

* * *

I offer special thanks to the noted author Konrad Bercovici,
who was ever helpful in the fight for Jewish liberation and
edited the English edition of this book.

I am indebted to the celebrated artist Arthur Szyk, who has
constantly supported the Jewish Underground and, graciously
contributed the drawing for the cover.

Acknowledgment is due to Mr. David Krakow for valuable
assistance in preparing the manuscript for publication, and to
the Jabotinsky Institute in Tel Aviv for its kind permission to
draw upon its collection of photographs.

ITZHAK GURION.
Chanukah 5710—December 1949.

Jewish Martyrs of Our Day

FROM 135 C.E., the year which marked the end of the
Bar Kochba revolt against the Roman Empire, until the
outbreak of the last World War, the Jewish people spilled
rivers of blood throughout the entire world. During close to
two thousand years of galut (diaspora) and wandering from
land to land, from pogrom to pogrom, the Jewish people brought
countless sacrifices in Europe, Asia and Africa.

Yet, from this long tradition of martyrdom there stands out
especially one heroic chapter, that of the Ten Martyred Rabbis
who were executed by the Romans and whose noblest representative was Rabbi Akiba. On the most sacred day of the year,
Yom Kippur, these Martyrs are recalled in a moving prayer.

The attitude of reverence for this chapter in the history of
Jewish martyrology derives from the fact that these Rabbis were
not just victims or mere fighters but that they represent the
spiritual aspect of the last Jewish revolt in our ancient history.

19

Rabbi Akiba ben Joseph, the last of the martyred Rabbis, had gathered around him, before he was taken captive by the Romans, more than twenty-four thousand young fighters. The martyrs of that era, therefore, have gone down in our history not only as martyrs alone but as battlers and revolutionaries who attempted to challenge a mighty empire, who fought and were killed in the struggle for the liberation of the Jewish people from Roman oppression.

More than eighteen centuries have passed since the Jewish people and its youth raised the banner of revolt. The *galut* with its enslavement, wanderings and pogroms became the order of the day. Great empires were destroyed and new empires arose but the Jewish *galut* continued down to our own generation when a revolt against another great empire, the British Empire, again erupted and this time ended in victory.

The recent revolt lasted only a few years. But it was a stormy and mighty one. Hundreds of soldiers of the Underground fell in battle and the revolt exacted also its toll of martyrs. Twelve were they in number, twelve young Jewish fighters imprisoned by British soldiers and led to the gallows by British hangmen. To these twelve, the Jewish national martyrs of our day, the following chapters are devoted.

Most of them I knew personally. I witnessed ten of the "trials" as liaison of the *Irgun Zvai Leumi* with the lawyers of the martyrs. It is too early to describe fully the greatness of their heroic lives and heroic deaths. Less than two years have passed since the day when the last three *Irgun* heroes went to the gallows with a song and with the blessing of *sheheheyanu* (Thanksgiving prayer)—"who has kept us alive, and has sustained us, and enabled us to reach this season." Less than eleven years have passed since the death of the first of the martyrs, Shlomo Ben Yosef. I still see him before me as he was dressed in red a few hours before the hangmen took him to the gallows: I recall vividly the youngish, short Eliahu Bet-Tzuri with his youthful smile as he appeared in my home during his school days, when he was already active in the youth groups of the national movement (*Huge Hanoar Haleumi*). I remember my walks with Dov Gruner on the Tel Aviv seashore and with Yaakov Weiss on the sand dunes between Nathanya and Ramat Tiomkin. And there was Yechiel Dresner, a frequent visitor at my home, always so quiet and so calm. I could not help imagining that before me there stood his deeply religious father who could not bring himself to raise his voice. And this young man was to become a great fighter. . . .

Many years will have to pass before we gain the proper perspective for evaluating their greatness, which is evident even in the minute details of their lives. However, we live in an age when history is being falsified. Shortsighted, partisan writers of the liberation history are endeavoring to rip the sacred pages of the latest Jewish revolt from the account of our struggle for freedom. On the other hand, we live at a time when the fight for final liberation must still be carried on and when this struggle for a bright tomorrow attracts also all those who remember the great *yesterday*.

I have made use of the time during which I am far from Israel and its daily struggles to draw but in broad strokes the portraits of the twelve national martyrs of our day. These chapters will serve merely as material for the future historian of our war for freedom. They contain only the dry facts and events which once caused every fibre of ours to quiver and every drop of our blood to boil.

THE AUTHOR.

The First in Two Thousand Years

(*Shalom Tabachnick—Shlomo Ben Yosef*)

THE BACKGROUND

ON April 19, 1936, there broke out in Palestine "Arab riots." It cannot be stressed too often that the Arabs would never have attempted to challenge Jewish strength if the British had not incited, encouraged and aroused them. Every attempt was part and parcel of the British intrigue against Zionism and its aims.

Somewhere in the secret offices where the British policy of intrigue is formulated, it was decided years ago, in the days following the Balfour Declaration, that the Jewish aims must not be realized. England was to maintain control over Jewish immigration into Palestine and to see to it that Jews never became a majority in their land.

Then came the years 1933-36 during which Hitler consolidated his rule over Germany. European Jews began to converge upon Palestine through every possible route. The British became apprehensive over the increase in Jewish population which grew within the course of a few years to a degree far exceeding the anti-Zionist plans. Fearing complete failure of their plans, the British Intelligence Service reverted to using its well-tried method of "divide and rule," which it had inherited from the Roman Empire. As a result, the "spontaneous Arab riots" broke out on April 19, 1936.

The official Jewish leadership often tried to find "suitable" names to describe these pogroms. They called them "riots," "disturbances," "regrettable incidents." However, the one word that could really describe this British intrigue—"pogroms," was studiously avoided. Hundreds of Jewish men, women and children were murdered in barbaric fashion and hundreds of thousands of dollars worth of goods were destroyed. Jewish fields were set afire throughout Palestine and thousands of saplings were uprooted, and still the official leadership hesitated to designate these barbaric actions by their right name— "pogroms."

Despite the warnings from all sides that the British and the Arabs were preparing something nefarious; despite the open telegrams which Vladimir Jabotinsky had sent to the High Commissioner about the situation as early as the beginning of March, 1936; despite Jabotinsky's warning to the official Jewish leadership that the "stench of the month of August, 1929, reaches my nostrils" (he referred to the pogroms which "broke out" at that time) ; despite all this, the official *Haganah* was prepared neither with arms nor with plans to make a strong stand against aggression.

When I speak of the "official *Haganah*," it should be noted that then there existed two sections in the *Haganah*. The largest and strongest section was composed of the socialist elements in the land. It was under the leadership and control of the official Jewish Agency. The second section, known as *Haganah Bet,* attracted the nationalist elements and was controlled by the so-called opposition to the Agency, headed by such men as Vladimir Jabotinsky, Pinchas Rutenberg, and others.

The British were naturally happy over the unpreparedness of the *Haganah.* Yet they felt that this situation would not long remain the same, that the growing bitterness might turn the bulk of the Haganah's rank and file toward the more radical elements. In order to forestall this development the British began to praise strongly the official Jewish leadership for its "highly ethical" conduct, thus trying to create the impression that such an attitude would be judged "ethically" and properly rewarded by the Government. . . . Sadly enough the official Jewish leadership was taken in by this hypocritical policy and decided to continue with the system of *havlagah,* of self-restraint and non-retaliation. It decided merely to engage in "self-defense," a practice which naturally could not prevent the slaughter of hundreds of victims, the shaming of Jewish women and the destruction of Jewish possessions.

In the circles of the *Haganah* and particularly in the ranks of *Haganah Bet* the sentiment grew against this policy. Protests began to be voiced that this system was playing into the hands of the British—by allowing the Arabs to make pogroms and thus inspiring European Jews with the fear that persecution awaited them not only in Germany but in Palestine as well. Nonetheless, the Jewish Agency succeeded in curbing the official

Haganah. Moreover, it succeeded in convincing some of the leaders of *Haganah Bet* that *havlagah* was the correct policy. This led to a split in the ranks of *Haganah Bet* and the more radical nationalist elements, especially the members of the New Zionist Organization under the leadership of Vladimir Jabotinsky, founded the *Irgun Zvai Leumi.* Jabotinsky appointed David Raziel head of the *Irgun.* Raziel at once proceeded to reorganize the fighting forces of the *Irgun* in order to enable it to carry out a retaliation policy. A few weeks after it was formed—on November 14th, 1937—the *Irgun* successfully carried out the first sporadic retaliatory actions against the Arab terrorists.

SHALOM TABACHNICK AT ROSH PINAH

It was an exceptionally dark night. In a tobacco warehouse in *Rosh Pinah,* a distant settlement in northern Galilee, a group of young *Betarim** sat at a table in a corner and carried on a quiet but spirited discussion. The small kerosene lamp which hung from the wall cast a dark, smoky light for a few feet. The rest of the large warehouse was in darkness. This, of course, was no deterrent to the discussion. The entire group was composed of members who were well known to each other. Also the two "guests" who had come from Tel Aviv to participate

---

* Members of the nationalist youth organization Brit Trumpeldor.

in the discussion were well known to the group. One could tell from the sound of the voice who the speaker was and in the semi-darkness the discussion was more intimate and appropriate.

The discussion centered around the timeliest questions of the day—the Arab-British pogroms, the harmful policy of *havlagah,* and the founding of the *Irgun.* It is noteworthy that it hardly touched upon the political side of the situation. Only one of the guests made mention of the British intrigue and the tense international situation which had begun to develop in the Mediterranean area following the Italian invasion of Ethiopia. Most of the young *Betarim* spoke of the shame of the pogroms, the shame occasioned when a son witnessed the murder of his old mother without retaliation, when a young father buried the charred body of his beloved child without taking revenge, when farmers watched their fields, their sweat and blood, go up in flames without organizing any opposition. The word *herpah* (shame) characterizes the spirit of that entire discussion. . . .

Suddenly the door of the warehouse was opened. In the darkness one could make out a young *Betari* who approached the table. The discussion was stopped to hear the young man report with a smile on his lips that a person, who claimed to be a *Betari,* had just arrived in the mess hall, that he was relating various unbelievable tales and wished to remain in the group. We understood that he really came to warn us to be more careful. . . .

The discussion had already been near conclusion before this interruption. We now rose, snuffed out the kerosene lamp, and started in the direction of the group quarters, which were located on the other side of the settlement. On such a dark night and coming from such a gathering, one had to be careful to find the road that led to the houses at the edge of the settlement, at the foot of Mt. Canaan on which stood the Arab village of *Djani.*

The mess hall was brightly lit. At a corner of the long table sat a broadboned young man who appeared tired and wet and wore badly torn shoes. I sat down next to him and told him my name in a very hushed voice, so that he should not catch it. . . . However, he spoke up, in a loud and clear voice. It was a remarkable tale that he related: he had come from Lutzk, Poland and was a *Betari* of long standing. Brought up in a poor family, he had to work from childhood on in order to help his parents. His evenings, however, he devoted to the *Betar* youth organization. Then came the pogroms in Palestine and he could not rest. He left his parents and work, and without a passport, visa or a penny to his name set out. A series of terrible and remarkable experiences were revealed to me, of smuggling across borders, traveling as an "illegal" immigrant aboard ship and finally Beirut, Lebanon. Some Greek fishermen who had set sail in a small boat for the shores of Palestine in order to fish there took him along. . . . But when he asked that they bring him a little further, they demanded money of him. Having none, they began to quarrel and he was cast overboard. He swam the small stretch of water and finally, crossing the Galilee hills, arrived at Naharia, thus fulfilling his life-long dream to be in Palestine in the *Betar* group of Rosh Pinah. . . . He wished to remain here. . . .

It was enough to look into his eyes to see that all he related was true. Afterwards I passed on my opinion to the members of the Rosh Pinah group. Shalom Tabachnick remained in the settlement.

SHLOMO BEN YOSEF

A few months later I saw him by chance at a meeting in Haifa. I had a short conversation with him on my way to the hotel. I already knew that he was an active member of the group at Rosh Pinah; not only a devoted and competent worker but also a leader in the social and cultural life there. I asked him what he was doing in Haifa. He replied sadly: "There is a great scarcity of work at Rosh Pinah because of the 'riots.' We cannot go out to work in the fields and my colleagues are beginning to feel the pinch of prolonged unemployment. I am young and healthy, so I have come to work in the Haifa port. . . . With my earnings of one day, ten to twelve members of Rosh Pinah can be fed."

Shlomo Ben Yosef (Shalom Tabachnik)
dressed in his Betar uniform.

He told me all this so simply and naturally that it seemed that it was the only way he could have acted. His eyes revealed that everything he had said was true but that there was an additional motive that had brought him to the port. . . . The thought occurred to me that perhaps he had come to procure arms for Rosh Pinah. This brought a smile to my lips which he seemed to understand. But apparently he did not want to discuss the matter. That day he was extra cautious. . . . I pressed his hand and we parted. . . .

That same year I had occasion to visit Rosh Pinah again a month or so before Passover. I came to take part in the funeral of a young *Betari,* Liberman, murdered by an Arab bullet in the fields of the colony. . . . With clenched fists and anger in their hearts the members accompanied him to his eternal rest at the foot of Mt. Canaan. . . .

On our way back from the funeral Shalom asked that I meet with him and two other friends for a short talk. He no longer bore the name Shalom Tabachnick. He was now *Shlomo Ben Yosef.* He spoke Hebrew fluently and was very prominent in the group. I went to meet them. I recognized both his friends whom I had known for some time. One was Abraham Shein (Ziv), who was still quite young, hardly more than seventeen. He too was born in Poland but had gone to Palestine as a child. In Tel Aviv he graduated from the Herzlia school and then went to join the *Betar* at Rosh Pinah. The other was Shalom Djuravin. Somewhat older than Shein, he was born of poor parents in Jerusalem. From childhood on he had to work to support himself. Later he became acquainted with *Betar* in Jerusalem, joined the organization and soon entered the Rosh Pinah group, the pride of the movement.

Our talk was quite a short one. Outside there waited the only automobile going to Tiberias. But much was said, particularly in the nature of a criticism born of pain and shame. "What will be the outcome?," they asked. They were unable to keep quiet any longer. . . . Now, what could I say in reply? Everything was still in its early stage. I knew something of the plans and preparations of the *Irgun*. But could I tell it to them? I realized that any separate, unprepared action would bring only harm. I tried to urge them to wait a bit longer and assured them that matters would come to a head but I myself felt I had not convinced them. . . . When the newspapers reported some five weeks later of an incident that occurred at Rosh Pinah, I could see the flashing, embittered eyes of the three. . . .

The incident was as follows:

During the first days of Passover, 1938, reports became current in the distant northern settlement of Rosh Pinah of an impending Arab attack. In the Arab village of *Djani,* located on Mt. Canaan and occupying a position overlooking Rosh Pinah, heated preparations were in evidence. The situation was tense. The reports became more alarming. All the fields of Rosh Pinah had been aflame for some days. The settlement was under great stress. The village of Djani was already preparing openly.

Without consulting anyone and without prior decision on the part of the Irgun leaders in the settlement or in Tel-Aviv, the three above-mentioned young men resolved to close off the way to Rosh Pinah at least to strange Arabs. They refused to allow strange Arabs to pass through the settlement unhampered.

During midday of Thursday, April 21, 1938 (Nissan 20, 5698), there appeared on the road from Safed to Rosh Pinah an Arab automobile carrying many strange Arabs who did not live in the neighborhood. The three young men stepped out on the road and tried to stop the automobile that approached Rosh Pinah. A single shot was fired and the Arabs fled in panic.

The British police, who for two years had stood by without raising a finger while Jews were cruelly murdered and Jewish fields were put to the torch, now became strangely "active." A few hours after the incident, the three young men were arrested. They gave themselves up without any struggle.

BRITISH PLANS

Despite the fact that not a single drop of blood was shed at Rosh Pinah and despite the fact that the police knew very well that the three young men had only fired into the air in order to discourage the Arabs from passing through the settlement, the British decided to create a big "terrorist" incident out of the Rosh Pinah affair. The very fact that Jews had resolved to withstand an Arab attack made them feel afraid. Their plan to frighten Jews from coming to Palestine would be endangered if Jews were to fight back. They knew very well that the Jews could put an end to the Arab "revolts" in a few days.

Regrettably enough, the official Jewish policy allowed itself to be taken in by the British intrigue. The day after the Rosh Pinah affair, the official bodies and their press were aroused. A wild and irresponsible agitation was begun against the "terrorists." This agitation made it possible for the British to prepare a big trial and to demand the severest penalty for the three Rosh Pinah "terrorists." No account was taken of the possible result of this agitation. The Jewish "official authorities" were merely concerned with keeping the Jewish youth from making any counter-attack. In order to frighten the embittered youth, beginning to show signs of disaffection, they were prepared to send some "terrorists" to the gallows.

The British understood all this. In addition to their intrigue between Arabs and Jews, they were now successful in bringing about a split between the Jews. In order to widen the split, they decided to go through with the hanging penalty. Thus on May 24, 1938, there began in Haifa the military "trial" of the first "Jewish terrorists."

PLAN OF DEFENSE

A quiet but basic dispute arose between the three young men in Acre prison and their friends on the outside during the weeks between the shooting in Rosh Pinah and the military "trial." Well-known jurists who followed the preparations of the police for the trial were of the opinion that the charge was a very weak one from a legal point of view. None of the three had been found at the scene of the shooting and arms were found not on but near them. Regarding Abraham Shein, the Polish consul declared that according to the report from his birth place he was still a minor. The greatest psychiatrist in Palestine agreed to declare that many years before, Shalom Djuravin had suffered from a high degree of nervousness which could recur under stress. They therefore thought that the defense should be conducted solely on a legal basis and that in this manner it would be possible to save all three from hanging.

Opposed to this approach were in the first place the three accused. Instinctively they felt that the British were merely looking for a chance to frighten the Jewish youth and that they would push through a death penalty for this purpose. They were aware that no legal efforts could avail in such a situation. Moreover, they had not committed their action haphazardly and did not wish to repudiate it and get off without a penalty. They had undertaken their action with the definite conviction that by such methods a breach could be made in the official policy of the *Haganah,* which under all circumstances wished to avoid Jewish retaliatory action. They were convinced that a Jewish offensive would not only wipe away the shame of pogroms in Palestine but would also put an end to British anti-Zionist intrigue and efforts to halt the large-scale immigration which was reaching the land through various avenues. To have conducted solely a legal defense would have meant a disregard of their conviction. They were prepared to appear before the British officers who called themselves "judges" and challenge them boldly. They were ready to expose British policy and take the consequences. The three accused were not even ready to accept the decision of the New Zionist Organization Executive in Palestine because they were aware that the younger members of that Executive were themselves against such a line of defense. This heroic stand, this act of open defiance—even more than the action itself—was a turning point in the history of the retaliatory fight.

It was during those difficult days that Professor Akzin came to Palestine as the emissary of Jabotinsky in order to appear before the Partition Commission and to demand that the boundaries of Palestine should include both sides of the Jordan. As Jabotinsky's emissary, Prof. Akzin expressed the opinion that the three young men should accept a legal defense on the understanding, however, that *the defense* would point up the political aspect of the "incidents" in Palestine.

THE TRIAL AND THE 'VERDICT'

The trial lasted for eleven days. It began on May 24 and the "verdict" was handed down on June 3. The legal defense was conducted by attorneys, Dr. Philip Joseph (a brother of Dr. Bernard Joseph of the regrettable Arlosoroff trial who today occupies a ministerial post in the Israeli Government) and Hoter-Yishai who was then a Revisionist and a member of the extreme wing of the party. He was chosen to assist Dr. Joseph in order to assure that Prof. Akzin's compromise formula for the defense would be maintained and carried out (Hoter-Yishai is now the prosecuting attorney of the Israeli army and has gained a sad reputation because of his conduct at the trial of the Stern Group leaders following the mysterious assassination of Count Bernadotte). Both attorneys exhibited great legal skill in the case. The testimony of all the witnesses brought by the British was disproved. The charge was masterfully refuted. Were this a normal civil case based on facts, the three would possibly have been entirely exonerated.

Left to right, Abraham Shein, Shalom Djuravin and Shlomo Ben Yosef at their "trial."

But this was a political "trial" before a military "court." Military officers require no facts. They need only a command.

And this they had received well in advance of the trial. The eleven-day "judicial" proceedings with their various testimonies and speeches served only as a front for back-room politics. Nothing availed. Neither the fine speeches nor the exposing of the pogroms against the Jews , nor even Dr. Joseph's statement before the officer-"judges" that ever since the destruction of the Temple no Jew had been hanged in Palestine. The "verdict" was handed down on the eve of Shavuot, June 3, 1938. Shlomo Ben Yosef and Abraham Shein were "sentenced" to hanging and Shalom Djuravin to life imprisonment until such time as he would be pardoned by the High Commissioner (he was freed three years later only to be re-arrested after a few months and sent to Latrun. Together with nineteen other prisoners, he escaped from there through a tunnel which they had themselves dug only to be re-arrested a second time and to begin his wanderings as a prisoner in Eritrea, Sudan and Kenya. . .). The sentenced young men accepted the "verdict" quite calmly. After the chairman of the "court" ended his official speech with the words: "I sentence you to the gallows and you will hang until dead . . .", Shlomo Ben Yosef arose and called out: "Long live the Jewish State on both sides of the Jordan."

AFTER THE 'VERDICT'

The sentenced remained calm but the Jewish world was outraged by this "verdict." The fact alone that Captain Robertson, the prosecutor for the British military, based his demand for the death penalty on the condemnations which the Agency and the *Vaad Leumi* had issued against the action of the three young men, aroused great bitterness amongst the Jews of Palestine. On the other hand, no Jew could bring himself to imagine that after two thousand years of *galut* there would be hanged in Palestine a Jew, a Jewish fighter for the liberation of his people and country. Although there were still two possibilities by which the two young men could be saved from the clutches of the British hangmen, either through a reversal of the "verdict" by the Commander-in-Chief of the British military forces in Palestine or through the granting of a pardon by the High Commissioner, none of those who understood the real causes of the verdict believed any longer that this would be done.

Only the Polish consul did not lose hope that he would be able to save Abraham Shein from the gallows. A special representative of his flew to Poland and brought back the official documents attesting that Shein had not reached his eighteenth birthday by April 21. All others like Dr. Weizmann, Chief Rabbi Herzog, the Polish Rabbis, the Wizo Organization and Jewish communities throughout the world merely asked for mercy from the British . But the latter were inured against all pleas. They were also certain that the official Jewish bodies— for whom *Havlagah* had become a fundamental philosophy of life—would continue to oppose retaliation, thus enabling the British to continue their intrigue against Jewish liberation.

This British feeling of assurance was made clear a few days later in a talk between the then Secretary for Colonies, Malcolm Macdonald and Vladimir Jabotinsky, who warned him that the hanging of Ben Yosef would arouse strong repercussions among the Jewish youth of Palestine and that this could lead to deeds which the British Government would deeply regret. Macdonald replied that he was certain that the official bodies controlled the entire Jewish youth and if a few "hot-heads" would try to break this control, they would be opposed by the entire Jewish youth and the official Jewish organizations.

ALL HOPE GONE

On June 25, the Commander-in-Chief of the British military forces in Palestine confirmed the "sentence" against Shlomo Ben Yosef and commuted the "sentence" of Abraham Shein to life imprisonment. General Haining, the Commander-in-Chief, apparently held the same opinion as Macdonald regarding the Jewish youth—they would remain quiet. But he was mistaken.

Only a few hours after this decision was made public, the police and military already had bloody work to do. Throughout the entire land protest demonstrations were held by hundreds of young people. On the streets of Tel-Aviv guns had to be used and dozens of people were wounded. The Government offices were flooded with requests for a pardon from all parts of the world, from Shanghai to New York from Warsaw to Capetown. The leftist elements in the country were also swept up by the pyschosis of making pleas to the High Commissioner. But they employed expressions which would have made it far better had they made no representations at all. Thus, for example, Dov Hos, the then vice-mayor of Tel-Aviv and one of the Haganah leaders stated: "This unfortunate person (Ben Yosef) who has made a mistake is worthy of mercy. . . ."

On June 27, Dr. Philip Joseph filed an appeal with the highest court in the land and stressed that he had secured new evidence on which basis he requested a second trial. He also asked that the court postpone the carrying out of the "sentence" until after a second trial. The very same day the court turned down his request. That evening all business and entertainment establishments were closed. Jews gathered for prayer in all synagogues. In the streets demonstrators marched and again there were wounded and arrests. . . . The air was heavy with panic and . . . revolt. In Tel Aviv and Jerusalem a "curfew" was declared but many streets were astir with embittered people.

Thus arrived the last day before the hanging, June 28. Early that morning Dr. Philip Joseph called the High Commissioner on the telephone and requested an appointment. The High Commissioner replied that he should send a letter and promised to give his answer the same day. . . . The *Vaad Leumi* issued a proclamation to the Jewish population to remain calm, to keep businesses open and to refrain from conducting demonstrations. At the same time, however, the Chief Rabbinate of Palestine appealed to the Jewish population to close all places of business and to gather in the synagogues to recite a special prayer which it had prepared. The pupils of the secondary schools ceased their studies on their own initiative and went into the streets. In Jerusalem the military again proclaimed a "curfew" and in Tel-Aviv thousands of people joined in demonstrations. . . .

And in Acre? Calmly and with a smile on his lips Shlomo Ben Yosef stood in his red clothes behind the bars of his death-cell and spoke with his close friends who had come to part with him. His was the smile of a person who had long bid farewell to this earth and had already been transported to the heavens above. With aching hearts we went to the death cell and for each of us Ben Yosef had a special smile and comforting word. . . . We wanted to tell him that all hope was not yet lost, but he pointed to the inscription which he had engraved on the wall of his death cell: *Tov lamut b'ad hamoledet* —it is good to die for the homeland, the same words which Joseph Trumpeldor had spoken before his heroic death, and he smiled. . . .

THE LAST NIGHT

The last night approached. . . . In a quarter of an hour we would all have to leave the death cell, the prison, and the city of Acre, and he would remain alone until the hanging. There were three of us who were to bid him final farewell—Menachem Arber, leader of the Palestine *Betar* organization, Dr. Samson Yunitchman, leader of the *Betar* group in Rosh Pinah and the writer. We entered the death cell with a feeling of sanctity and sadness. But Ben Yosef did not permit any show of grief. He wanted to know what the *Irgun Zvai Leumi* had decided. We informed him that the *Irgun* had decided to forgive his failure to consult anyone before acting and that it had appointed him an officer of the *Betar* group at Rosh Pinah. His face lit up with an inner glow and arising to salute us he said: *"Fine. But I should like to know if the counter-attack which I began will continue."* Our affirmative reply called forth a deep-felt joy. He turned to the inscription, *"It is good to die for the homeland"* and again saluted. I told him that his aged mother had sent a telegram to the High Commissioner requesting that the execution be delayed because she wanted to embrace him once more before the hanging. . . . For a moment he was overcome by grief. He loved his mother dearly. . . . But soon his eyes lit up again—he loved Palestine and its freedom more than anything else, even more than his own youthful life. . . .

Nightfall approached. The gates of the Acre fortress swung shut. Only he and his hangmen remained there. . . . Our chauffeur drove us quickly to Tel-Aviv. During these last hours we still clung to the hope that all was not lost. . . . The High Commissioner still had to give his reply. . . . Jabotinsky in London was to see some ministers that day. . . . And the

The courtyard of Acre Prison; in the foreground is Zeev (Vladimir) Jabotinsky during his internment in 1920.

streets were filled with Jewish demonstrators. In Jerusalem a crowd of women demonstrators broke through the police lines and went to the palace of the High Commissioner. In Tel Aviv there were already dozens of wounded, even among the British. . . . Near the meeting-place of the Tel Aviv *Betar,* a struggle broke out between the police and the *Betarim* and dozens were arrested. Hundreds were gathered near the headquarters of the New Zionist Organization. They waited for word. Perhaps Jabotinsky would call from London. Permission was granted for a special emissary of Dr. Philip Joseph to transmit a letter to the High Commissioner. . . . But he returned at dawn. The High Commissioner could not intervene. . . .

The Chief Rabbinate still tried. A Rabbi had been ordered to come to the fortress to recite the *viddui* (confession) with Shlomo Ben Yosef. The Rabbinate replied that this day was Rosh Hodesh (the New Moon of the month *Tammuz*) and that according to Jewish tradition this was a holiday—a minor holiday but a holiday nevertheless—and the laws of the land ruled out executions on any festival of the three official religions. The Rabbinate therefore wished to apply pressure to delay the execution for another day. . . . Perhaps. . . . But the British hangmen could wait no longer. . . . Should no Rabbi agree to come to say the *viddui* with Shlomo Ben Yosef, he would go to the gallows without it. . . .

The only Jewish officer in the Acre fortress assumed guard on that last night. He thought that he might be able to comfort him, whom all loved and revered for his heroism. He stood amazed near the death cell. . . . Shlomo Ben Yosef slept calmly, with a smile about his lips. . . . When he later arose, he requested some water and washed himself carefully. . . . The officer was astounded at his calmness. . . . A little later the officer brought him civilian clothes, a white shirt and clean trousers. Ben Yoself told him that he was promised his *Betar* uniform for the hanging and that he would not go willingly if he were refused the uniform. The officer was well acquainted with British sergeants. . . . He knew that this could cause a struggle and wanted to avoid it. He told Ben Yosef that he would be dragged by force to the gallows and that this would be interpreted as a sign that he was in great fear before his death. . . . Ben Yosef reconsidered a moment and said: "Very well, I will go. Let it not be said that a Jewish soldier is afraid of death." But the officer had to promise that he would tell his friends, so that they might forgive his going to the gallows without his *Betar* uniform. . . . The officer recited a few psalms with him. . . . The sun rose on the day of June 29, 1938 (30 Sivan, 5698), as Ben Josef marched to the gallows. . . . From the corridor which led from the death cell to the gallows could be heard his voice: *"Yechi Jabotinsky"!* (Long live Jabotinsky) "Lamut o lichbosh et Hahar"! (to die or to take the mountain) and followed by the song of *Hatikvah*. The Jewish prisoners at Acco, including his two friends who stood "trial" with him, arose and joined in the singing. . . . A few moments later they sang alone. Shlomo Ben Yosef had already been hanged. . . .

AFTER THE HANGING

That same dawn two small autos stood at the crossroads leading from *Haifa* to *Acre*. In one of the machines sat the Rabbi of Haifa. The Chief Rabbinate had decided that if the British would go through with the hanging, he should go to say the *viddui* with Ben Yosef. In the other machine sat Ben Yosef's closest friends and representatives of the Jabotinsky movement. They had received permission the day before to come to Acre and wished to be at the funeral. . . . But a British officer blocked the road. The Rabbi protested and so did the others but the officer had but one reply: "curfew." After much effort he went to call Acre. He returned with the message, "it's all over . . ." Rabbi Marcus drove back to Haifa and we to Rosh Pinah. . . .

In Tiberias the road was again blocked off—"curfew." Prof. Akzin, who accompanied us, tried to intervene with the British Governor of Tiberias but to no avail. The Governor could not get us permission to proceed to Rosh Pinah but we could make a private telephone call there. Hastily each of us wrote down his words. Prof. Akzin in the name of Jabotinsky, Menachem Arber in the name of the Palestinian *Betar*. When I took up the telephone to speak in the name of the various nationalist organizations, I said the following:

"In the relations between the Jewish people and England there will always remain . . . the gallows. The nationalist organizations promise at the sacred grave to fulfill his wish—they will fight."

An hour later I again stood at the gate of Acre fortress. I bargained with the British sergeant to give me the official communique regarding the hanging. He agreed to for a few pounds and I hurried off to *Tel-Aviv*. I returned to a silent city. All businesses were shut and the streets were empty. But toward evening stormy demonstrators marched and their marching forebode the spilling of blood, and the struggle for national freedom.

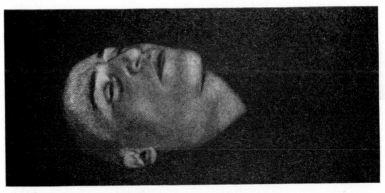

Shlomo Ben Yosef after his execution.

After the passing of only five days from the time of the hanging, Macdonald knew that not he but Jabotinsky had been right when the latter warned that the Jewish youth would not overlook the hanging. In every country where there were Jewish

David Raziel, first leader of the
Irgun Zvai Leumi

masses, the windows of the British consulates were shattered.
In Palestine itself there occurred the first great explosions
which indicated that the *Irgun* had begun to fight. This
was but the beginning of a struggle that exposed British intrigue, which continued despite arrests, despite denouncement by
the official Jewish bodies, despite the fact that all the Palestine
prisons were already well filled. Nothing frightened the Irgun
youth and its first commander, David Raziel. The struggle
continued until the outbreak of World War II against Nazi
Germany. At that time the *Irgun* declared an armistice which
prevailed until revoked by Menachem Beigin in January, 1944,
when he proclaimed the open revolt against the British occupying
forces in Palestine.

In the Nest of Intrigue

C AIRO, the capital of Egypt, had long been the center of British intrigue in the Near East. A short time after World War I, an Egyptian revolt broke out against British domination and England had to agree to certain "compromises." As is usually the case when England makes "compromises," she yielded her control only outwardly. In her dealings with backward people, she would ostensibly agree to their independence but retain her army in the country for one reason or another and thus remain the actual ruling force. In Egypt there were various "reasons": her interests in the Suez Canal and her "colony", the Sudan.

Thus was Egypt "liberated." She has her own King, ministers and parliament and all the trimmings. But British soldiers remain in Port Said near the Suez and in Khartoum near the Sudan and England constantly holds a whip over Egypt. When during World War II, the Egyptian King refused to comply with British demands, the British *ambassador* paid a "visit" to the palace in Cairo, accompanied by British tanks and soldiers. . . . Eventually the King granted the British "requests." This is the nature of Egyptian independence.

But Cairo was not merely the center of intrigue for Egypt alone. From there the network of British intrigue reached out far beyond the boundaries of Egypt. Here were the headquarters of the general staffs of the British Middle East forces and the Intelligence Service. The network reached out as far as India and Ethiopia in the south and the Balkans in the north. In this cauldron of intrigue were also concocted the Palestine policy, the Arab League, and the anti-Zionist and anti-Jewish measures. Here was to be found the key that closed the gates of Palestine, so that any Jew who sought escape from the Nazi gas chambers was unable to reach his country. In Cario were formulated devilish plans against the Jewish center in Palestine and the emergence of a free Jewish State.

THE IRISH 'PATRIOT'

During World War II, it was Lord Moyne who was in charge of British intrigue. Ostensibly, he had the rank of a government official but the highest British official in Cairo was also the highest officer of the so-called Intelligence Service for the entire Middle East.

Lord Moyne's record was full of intrigue. Irish by birth, he nevertheless helped the British in their fight against an independent Ireland. The Lordship which he received from the British crown led him to betray his own homeland and made him responsible for the death of thousands of Irish fighters. Even after England was forced to agree to the establishment of a separate Irish Republic, Lord Moyne was among the leading adherents of Irish partition, and North Ireland—Ulster—has remained—to this day—a whip over Ireland and a basis for strained relations between the two countries. . . .

It was this Irish "patriot" who was placed at the head of British intrigue against every Zionist aspiration during the war years. He was the source of opposition to the formation of a Jewish Army. He blocked the landing of the *Struma*, a boat that carried 800 Rumanian Jews, who had escaped from Rumania a few days before the Nazi occupation only to find no haven and eventually to go down at sea. Lord Moyne was the one who ordered the Jewish refugees on the ship *Atlantic*, which had run the British blockade, to be sent to the Isle of Mauritius where dozens died of African fever. He was also responsible for the deaths of over 200 Jews who were caught on the ship *Patria* in Haifa bay and who blew it up themselves in order not to be deported to Mauritius.

THE CRIME AND THE PUNISHMENT

At one o'clock on November 6, 1944, when Lord Moyne returned in a small military automobile from his office to his mansion home, located in the wealthy neighborhood of Cairo—*Zamalek*, two persons in civilian clothes approached the automobile and fired at him. One bullet wounded him in the neck and another near the lungs. The chauffeur, a soldier, tried to shoot at the two assailants and was killed immediately. Lord

Moyne's private secretary, Lady Ausbrun, and his adjutant Captain Yosenslaw, who were with him in the auto, escaped unscathed.

The Captain together with an Egyptian policeman pursued the assaliants and caught them on the Balok bridge. They soon discovered that the two men were not Egyptians but were unable to exact any information from them. At 11 o'clock that night Lord Moyne died despite the extraordinary efforts of the doctors to save him. The Egyptian Prime Minister *Ahman Mahar Pasha,* who was also Commander-in-Chief of the Army (he was assasinated in 1946 by an Egyptian), immediately called a special meeting of the cabinet and himself assumed charge of the investigation.

The refusal of the two assasins to make any kind of statement at the first interrogation naturally rendered more difficult the task of the Egyptian police and British Intelligence Service. But a number of clues were self-evident. Their Arab speech was very poor and the only language in which they could adequately express themselves was Hebrew. . . . Later their photographs were published and various people reported to the police establishing their identity. Their temporary address was discovered and their passports were found. The first official police communique stated that the two were *Moshe Itzhak Cohen* and *Hayim Saltzman.* It was clear that they were from Palestine.

INCITEMENT TO FRATRICIDAL WAR

Even before it became known that the two were members of any underground group, Churchill expressed himself in Parliament against the entire Yishuv. The official bodies, like the

Jewish Agency and the Vaad Leumi (National Council), immediately declared:

> "The horrible crime, which was committed outside the boundaries of Palestine and whose circumstances are still unknown and unclear, again demonstrates the great danger from the terrorist group which still exists in Palestine.
>
> "The terror in the land endangers our political work and can destroy our inner peace. The *Yishuv* (Jewish Community) is called upon to eliminate this group from its midst, to deny it protection or support, to disdain its threats and to help the British in every way possible to uproot their organization and prevent acts of terror. . . ."

On November 10, the British Intelligence Service, together with the Palestine British police who had been called to Cairo,

Eliahu Hakim

discovered the identity of the men who went under the name of Moshe Cohen and Hayim Saltzman. The real name of the first was Eliahu Hakim. His father lived in Haifa and his family consisted of three brothers and a sister.

The second was found to be Eliahu Bet-Tzuri, who lived together with his father and two sisters in Tel-Aviv. Born in

Eliahu Bet Tzuri

Jerusalem, he graduated from secondary school there and began his studies at the Hebrew University. His father was a high-ranking official in the Tel-Aviv post office. Both young men stated that they were members of the Stern Group known as the *Lochmei Cherut Yisroel* (Fighters for the Freedom of Israel) and that it was by the decision of their group that they shot at Lord Moyne, who is "an enemy of Israel."

Dr. Weizmann was called in to see Prime Minister Churchill on November 11, and immediately thereafter left for Palestine. Upon his arrival, a terrible and disastrous struggle ensued between the Jews of Palestine. Any young man suspected of being a member of the Stern Group or *Irgun* was handed over to the British police. Yet the British were still unsatisfied. Churchill demanded in Parliament that the Jews liquidate the Underground. This would have been tantamount to civil war. The official bodies sensing that their own position was highly endangered by the growing sympathy toward the "revolt" were prepared for this tragic eventuality.

CIVIL WAR AVERTED

Despite the dangerous agitation of Weizmann and *Ben Gurion,* who put the problem before a special conference of the Labor Federation as "either we or they," and despite the demand of all the newspapers to "destroy" the underground, a demand which would have meant the arming of brother against brother, the agitation fell through. There were a number of reasons for this.

1) The Underground had decided not to retaliate against Jews. It was difficult for the Underground to order its members to refrain from returning blow for blow. But the devotion of the Underground soldiers was so great that they obeyed even this difficult order and did not retaliate.

2) It was only a few months thereafter that the *Irgun* proclaimed its revolt. The broad masses of the population, including many members of the *Haganah,* had inner sympathy for the Underground. The disappointing results of the Jewish Agency's

appeasement policy towards the British considerably weakened its hold on the Yishuv. All the efforts of British secret agents to foment civil war, were to no avail. The *Yishuv* overwhelmingly rejected collaboration. Following the first wave of denunciations which led to the arrest of several hundred Underground fighters, the Yishuv turned away in disgust from the collaborators.

3) Only three weeks had passed since Lord Moyne's death when the British put an end to the demands of the official bodies and "public opinion" for civil war. On November 28 a military "court" convicted two members of the *Haganah,* David Epstein and David Solomon, who had been found carrying arms. Despite the fact that Eliahu Golomb, the *Haganah* chief at that time, appeared as a witness and declared that the two young men were opposed to terror and that the police had known of the arms, they were "sentenced" to seven years imprisonment. . . . At that juncture, it was a severe "sentence." This opened the eyes of many in the *Yishuv* to the reality that the British were, in fact, bent not upon eradicating "terrorism" but upon the suppression of any attempt to oppose their oppressive policies. The desire for civil war was lessened considerably, although the agitation continued for many weeks. This irresponsible agitation was a factor in bringing the two Underground fighters of Cairo to the gallows.

PRESSURE ON EGYPT

England was not satisfied with its pressure on the official Zionist bodies. She also put pressure on the Egyptian governmental agencies. The two fighters awaited their trial and according to Egyptian law they were to have been brought before a civil court. This did not please the British who knew that a civil court would not be dependent upon British will. They were afraid of an open trial which would give the fighters a chance to defend themselves and expose the British intrigue in Palestine and Egypt. They also wanted revenge in the form of the death penalty. A civil court might have imposed a prison sentence.

Extreme pressure was applied to have the case tried before a military court. On January 4, 1945, the prime minister, who was also the army commander, announced that Eliahu Hakim and Eliahu Bet-Tzuri would be tried before a military court. Various protests were voiced against the decision of the Egyptian government. The Lawyer's Association in Cairo also protested the action. The broad masses in Egypt were opposed to British intrigue in the country. The intelligentsia had always felt that these intrigues were placing Egypt still more under British domination (the war against Israel proved to them that neither the Egyptian King nor his ministers ruled Egypt but the British ambassadors). All these protests, however, were of no avail. The small feudal group which rules Egypt with British help, against the will of the people, took little account of public opinion even in internal matters. It decided the two Palestinian fighters would receive none other than a military "trial," to take place on January 10, 1945.

The Lawyer's Association, however, did not forego its protest. It enlisted the greatest and finest lawyers for the defense. *Tufik Dos Pasha,* who served as Minister of Justice during the *Wafd* (Egyptian national party) Government, offered his services as defense attorney. *Ali Bedui Pasha,* a member of the law faculty of the Cairo University, also offered his services.

Such lawyers as *Hassan Bey Hasni* and *Hassan Bey Gwadui,* who are considered leaders in the Egyptian legal profession, also volunteered. A British citizen who had a large legal practice in Egypt, Golding, also offered to aid the defense. If the English Government thought that it could avoid a public political trial, it was mistaken. With such a brilliant defense corps it was no wonder that dozens of correspondents from leading European and American newspapers came to Cairo especially for the trial.

LIFE AND DEATH STRUGGLE

The British were also busy with preparations for the "trial." The military "judges" were designated according to their request. The choice for prosecuting attorney was an old-time lackey, who had acquired his position, thanks to the British and his collaboration with them, *Ebed Al Rahman Tvir.* The charge contained five points. One was an accusation of premeditated murder, that is, a demand for the death penalty.

On January 10, 1945, the military "court" began its sessions. *Tvir* explicitly and openly demanded the death penalty. In a statement Eliahu Bet-Tzuri demanded an international court.

"This trial," he said, "is too broad in its implications to be confined within the boundaries of Egypt alone." But the "court" rejected his demand. The defense then requested that the trial be delayed in order to allow more time for preparation but this too was rejected. But the greatest sensation of the first day was the refusal of the only Palestinian Jewish lawyer to take part in the defense.

for many weeks the Hakim family had worked to secure
permission for the Palestinian lawyer, A. L. Sall to defend their
son. According to Egyptian law, no foreign attorney can appear before an Egyptian court. Nevertheless, permission was
received for Sall to take part in the trial in order to "assist" the
Egyptian lawyer. The British police in Palestine, who had
refused to issue Sall any passport suddenly "agreed" and per-

Eliahu Hakim, standing, is speaking at his
"trial" in Cairo, Seated is Eliahu Bet Tzuri.

mitted him to leave the country. On the first day of the
trial he declared that "he thanked the judges for their permission but . . . his clients refused to accept his line of defense and
he therefore had to withdraw. . . ." It was clear that A. L. Sall
demanded that his clients should refrain from making a political
trial out of the case. . . .

The Egyptian lawyers proceeded differently and with more respect for human freedom. They conducted the trial according to the wishes of the two defendants and it is quite possible that they accepted the case primarily because of its political character. . . . They brought the recent British White Paper on Palestine before the court and declared with pathos: *"This document was a heavy blow for the Jews. The Jewish youth drew the only obvious conclusion—'you gave us hope and withdrew it.' The terrible tragedy of the Jewish people in recent years influenced the Jewish youth."* They recalled the Schwarzbard and Frankfurter cases; the first having assassinated Petlura, the leader of the Ukraine pogroms, and the second having shot the Nazi vice-Consul in Switzerland, and the decisions of the respective Courts against capital punishment. They mentioned the Nazi gas chambers and declared: "No wonder that young Jews lost their equilibrium during such years."

But of what avail human words and legal brilliance when the "sentence" was decided in advance, when it was determined not in the "court" but in the political offices of the British ruling clique in Egypt. On January 18, the "court" declared that the "file" of the case was being transferred to the office of the Cairo *Mufti* (highest territorial Moslem authority) . . . (according to Egyptian law, no judges can inflict the death penalty without the consent of the highest religious authority. But it has never happened that the *Mufti* should challenge the sentence of a court).

Two days later, on January 20, the last session of the trial was held and the "judges" announced that the *Mufti* had confirmed their decision and that it was . . . the death penalty.

Both fighters, Eliahu Hakim and Eliahu Bet-Tzuri, received the "sentence" with a smile. Bet-Tzuri told an American correspondent: *"Naturally I would like to live but not at the price of my Jewish honor."* The strained atmosphere lasted for a few weeks during which petitions were filed with the Prime Minister and the Minister of Justice (according to Egyptian law, one cannot apply directly to the king for a pardon but must go through the office of the Minister of Justice who must first sign the plea). However, the British "ambassador" in Cairo blocked all pleas.

In the beginning of March, 1945, it was already clear that British pressure on the Egyptian king and his minister had been crowned with "success." Despite all this, the Egyptian regime was more tolerant than the Palestinian government in those days. Both brothers of *Eliahu Hakim* and both sisters of *Eliahu Bet-Tzuri* were granted permission to come to Cario to see them. On March 21, when it was already known that the two heroic fighters would be hanged the next morning—the members of their families were granted permission to see them. . . .

At 8 A.M. on Thursday, March 22, 1945, the Egyptian hangmen, following British orders, led the two Jewish Underground fighters to the gallows. Not a single Jew was present. No one knows the details of that last night of the two Jewish heroes in a strange city and a foreign land as they counted the last minutes of their young lives. But one thing was clear to all: they went to the gallows with the same proud feeling of the noble fighters, who had gone before them and the noble fighters who followed them . . . with faith in the forthcoming victory over the tyrannical British rule in Palestine.

No more than three years ensued from their last night and British rule in Palestine was broken and destroyed. The Underground fought and won.

TWO UNDERGROUND HEROES SAVED
FROM THE GALLOWS

Michael Ashbel   Yosef Simchon

Saved From the Gallows*

THE month of March, 1946, was one of a period of ten months during which the *Irgun* was able to conduct its revolt against British oppression in Palestine with a greater degree of calmness. From November, 1945, to July, 1946, the *Haganah* joined in the war against the British and, was a part of the *Tnuat Ha-Meri* (Resistance Movement) which en-

---

* This chapter deals with the two Underground heroes, Itzhak Ashbel and Yosef Simchon, who were under the threat of hanging for a number of weeks but were saved from this fate by the *Irgun*. Because the "verdict" issued against them was the first that led the *Irgun* to retaliate by imprisoning British officers, I decided to include the chapter. It helps to illustrate the story of Jewish martyrdom in our day.

compassed besides the *Irgun,* the Fighters for the Freedom of Israel (Stern Group). True, this agreement included a certain number of reservations which limited the *Irgun* in its battle, but it also had many positive points.

That the entire Jewish youth was united in the struggle against British power was in itself an important factor in the fight for liberation. Had the *Haganah* not withdrawn later from the struggle, victory might have come sooner and the area of the State of Israel might have been much greater today. We could have avoided all the British intrigues in the United Nations for those two years during which commission followed commission and delay was the order of the day.

The second positive point consisted in the fact that the *Irgun* was able to concentrate entirely on the British front. Prior to November, 1945, and after July, 1946, the *Irgun* had to be more apprehensive of the *Haganah* spies in all its military action than of the British secret police. The *Haganah* had in its employ hundreds of spies who followed members of the *Irgun* and Stern Group and investigated every suspicious movement and arms cache. Many thousands of dollars collected all over the world in order to arm the *Haganah* were spent in spying on the Underground. Only strict and effective secrecy prevented many failures during those years. But even secrecy could not prevent the arrest of dozens of high-ranking officers and hundreds of men by the British police with the aid of the *Haganah.* Often they were taken into custody with the arms which the *Haganah* spies had found in their possession.

The third positive point of the agreement was that it contributed to the morale of the *Irgun* and influenced its discipline. There had been great bitterness in *Irgun* ranks against the spy system by which Jewish fighters were handed over to the British forces. This bitterness could have also given rise to grumbling against the *Irgun* Command which used every disciplinary means to control the anger of the men and their desire to retaliate. . . . In those dark days the *Irgun* fully realized that every retaliatory measure could bring about the civil war for which the British were waiting. Only the abiding faith which the *Irgun* soldiers and officers had in their leaders was able to prevent counter-attacks against spies and collaborators which might have precipitated civil war.

The decision of the *Haganah* in November, 1945, to enlist in the struggle, albeit with some reservations, strengthened the faith of the soldiers in their leaders' intuition which foresaw even in the most critical days that the *Haganah* youth would eventually join in the war of liberation. The agreement therefore infused great enthusiasm into the *Irgun* ranks. The fact that those who hitherto kept aloof now joined in the fight strengthened the faith of the soldiers in their leaders' foresight.

There was still another positive point in the agreement: it left the *Irgun* a free hand in procuring arms. At the beginning of the negotiations, the *Haganah* made the generous suggestion that the budget of the combined struggle be borne by the united movement. It thought that its large financial means would impress the *Irgun* which had always had a small treasury. However, the *Haganah* was mistaken. Despite the enthusiasm with which the *Irgun* viewed the participation of the *Haganah* in the struggle, it seriously doubted whether the latter would carry the struggle to its culmination. Indeed nine months later, after the first blow at the hands of the British, the *Haganah* withdrew. It was a good thing that the *Irgun* never gave up its right to possess its own arms and conduct its own financial campaigns for acquiring them. It proved wise and farsighted.

What primarily caused the *Irgun* to reject the bid of the *Haganah* to set up a common budget, was the *Irgun* opinion that arms should be captured by force from the British and their army camps. It pointed to the danger of the British handing over their ammunition stores to the Arabs. It therefore suggested that the joint military plans include attacks on military camps for the purpose of confiscating arms.

Three years later, in August, 1948, Ben Gurion disclosed the "secret" that at the time of the proclamation of the Jewish State and the invasion of Palestine by the Arab countries, the *Haganah* had but few arms. The *Irgun* had known this "secret" for a long time. What Ben Gurion naturally kept quiet was the scandalous fact that despite the millions which the *Haganah* had raised throughout the world for decades, it was empty-handed when the fateful day came. Ben Gurion also kept another thing quiet: that he himself was responsible for the *Haganah* having "so few arms" (while the Arabs had so much). As early as August, 1945, the *Irgun* advanced plans for attacks against British military camps in order to capture arms by force. Had the *Haganah* accepted the proposal, the Jews would have had enough arms and conversely—the Arabs would have had little. . . . But Ben Gurion refused to consider it.

And the *Irgun* went ahead on its own. Besides taking part in joint actions, it successfully carried through a series of arms confiscations in a number of large British army camps. The *Irgun* units "visited" many military camps and acquired a large quantity of arms. One of the biggest actions was against the huge military camp in Sarafand, not far from Ramleh and Lydda.

'BRITISH SOLDIERS'

On March 6, 1946, a convoy of British trucks drew up before the iron gate of the military camp at Sarafand. The trucks were empty except for a few officers and soldiers. These were *Irgun* men who had disguised themselves as Britishers. At the gate, the commander of the convoy handed the guard a written permit to enter the camp. He also presented him with an order from the highest British military command to transfer to the convoy a certain quantity of arms. All the documents of course had been "drawn up" by the *Irgun*. But they were prepared so expertly that neither the guard nor the camp commander had any cause to suspect their genuineness. The conduct of the *Irgun* soldiers was so natural and calm that the British officers invited them into the camp's canteen for a drink and the British soldiers helped them load the arms on the *Irgun* truck. Only after the quantity of arms taken was observed to be far in excess of that requested in the order, and the *Irgun* soldiers kept on loading, did the commander become suspicious. . . . But it was too late. All telephone and telegraph connections between the camp and the outside had been cut off. The *Irgun* soldiers were armed while the British stood helplessly by in their own camp. . . .

When the trucks were completely filled, the *Irgun* officer who was in command of this confiscation ordered that explosives be placed under the remaining arms and warned the British that they would soon be detonated. The British now had only one thought —to get as far as possible from the fearful explosion. The *Irgun* soldiers were free to drive out of the camp and remove the arms with the greatest of speed. When the explosion took place, the trucks already were some distance from the camp. A few *Irgun* units remained in the area to prevent pursuit of the trucks until they reached their destination.

One of the units met up with some British troops that rushed to Sarafand when they heard the explosion. They skirmished and the small *Irgun* unit succeeded not only in gaining time

Irgun soldiers examining arms captured from the British. The man in the center is Yosef Simchon's brother.

but in withdrawing in good order. Only two men were wounded and they were removed in a small car accompanied by two *Irgun* nurses, who were always on duty whenever a unit went into action. The British, however, immediately proclaimed a "curfew" over the roads surrounding Sarafand. Although they failed to retrieve the arms, they did capture the two wounded men and their nurses. The nurses, Ziporah Flumen and Shulamit Shmueli, were sent to the Bethlehem concentration camp for women and the wounded men were sent to the prison hospital in Jerusalem.

The wounded were: Itzhak Michael Ashbel, twenty-four years old, a poetic soul with literary ability. He was the author of the Hebrew poem *Ale Barikodot* (see Page 82), which later became the most popular song of the Underground. The second was Yosef Simchon, nineteen years old, one of the outstanding *Irgun* heroes during the years of its underground activities and today an officer in the Israeli army.

It took many weeks before they recovered from their wounds. The British decided to try them before a military "court." The *Irgun* consulted the prisoners regarding the line of defense they wished to pursue. Any *Irgun* soldier who fell into the hands of the British had a choice between two alternatives. One was to deny any participation in the fight or any adherence to the *Irgun* and to pretend that he just happened to be an innocent bystander at or near the battle scene. The second alternative— and this was the one almost invariably adopted by the *Irgun* soldiers—was to declare openly that he was a soldier of the *Irgun,* that he considered himself a prisoner of war and did not recognize the legality of British rule in Palestine and the competence of a British court to sit in judgment on Hebrew citizens in their own homeland.

The *Irgun* High Command never presumed to debate which line of defense should be adopted in any particular case. The prisoner himself had to decide in this matter of life and death and to make his own choice. There was a case in which five *Irgun* soldiers were taken prisoner by the British and three declared that they were soldiers of the *Irgun,* while the two others chose to plead not guilty. Though it was clear that this might aggravate the position of the former (they were hanged a

few months later) and although the two who pleaded not guilty
stated that if the High Command of the Irgun did not approve
of their attitude they would submit to its decision and alter their
line of defense, they were nevertheless given a free hand and all
the legal assistance they needed.

Max Kritzman, who frequently served as defence council for captured Irgun soldiers.

Ashbel sent the following reply in the name of Simchon and
in his own name through their lawyer, Max Kritzman:

> "I received your inquiry regarding our 'trial' which is to
> be held shortly and I have decided to conduct myself as
> becomes a Jewish fighter who has been reared in the spirit
> of the *Irgun* and whose aim it is to serve the struggle for

liberation to the end. I want to be of service even through the last opportunity I now have of boldly bringing the *Irgun* message to the public.

"I hope my 'trial' will facilitate the realization of the aim for which I have fought and fallen. You are making a mistake if you wish merely to safeguard my life. I have been in danger more than once and always I have felt that only thus could I fulfill my duty as a soldier. One must not think of one's personal fate. The fate of my people has always been uppermost in my mind.

"I beg you to inform my superiors that I am ready to bear my punishment with courage and pride. It will be easier for me to take the consequences if I feel that I have done my duty."

THE 'TRIAL'

On June 12, the two *Irgun* soldiers were brought before British officers who called themselves a "military court" and did not even know their own code of law. They required no legal charge. They knew only that they had received their orders from their superiors. . . . The whole "court" was merely a pretense. Counsellor Max Kritzman immediately withdrew and Ashbel made the following declaration:

"I admit nothing and do not recognize any guilt. I do not wish to enter into a debate with my accusers or the 'court.' I do not wish to defend myself. I do not wish to cross-examine the witness nor do I desire to put or answer any questions. I do not recognize your laws, in the same way that any freedom-loving citizen refuses to accept a system which has made his country one large prison, its citizens prisoners or candidates for the gallows and its rulers hangmen. We know the reason why your superiors have instituted this reign of terror. They want to break the spirit of our people which is fighting with its last ounce of strength for its existence and the future of its children.

They want to force us to accept the fate which the secret British offices have decreed—the fate of a scattered and enslaved people which can be slaughtered and trodden underfoot. They want to frighten us, to destroy our unity and weaken our preparedness. However, all your efforts are in vain. Your rulers should have learned from history—their own and that of other peoples—that one cannot annul the laws of God and man with tyranny, and that by barbaric methods, no matter how extreme, one cannot suppress a just aim and longing for freedom. They should have known that every such attempt calls forth efforts to retaliate. They should have known that in the relations between peoples and particularly those between the nations of the world and Israel, there is no wrong that goes unpunished. If despite this, your rulers have robbed our land and have introduced into it barbaric and tyrannical laws, it can only mean that God has deprived them of their senses and blinded them in order to remove them from the scene.

"Be it as it may, you will not break the will of the Jewish people, nor destroy the desire for liberation which fills the hearts of all its sons. The statement I make here will serve as one example among many others that you will be unable to break the will of 600,000 Jewish citizens who are united as one in the struggle for the liberation of their land from bloody British rule. . . ."

'YOU WILL NOT DESTROY US'

The "court" session lasted no more than one day. The British officers made no attempt even to imitate legitimate judges. At the conclusion of these proceedings Yosef Simchon declared:

"I do not want to enter into any of the details of the charge which my accusers have brought here. Although I can do so, I do not want to prove that the procedure by which your witnesses have 'recognized' me was staged from beginning to end and that I have no connection with all the things which have been written into the charge. It is a fact that your representatives who wear the uniform of the British police tried to make me 'confess' by the use of medieval torture and Gestapo methods. They investigated me while I was still wounded and despite my condition— and perhaps because of it—brought me to their inquisition chamber, beat me barbarously and warned that they would kill me if I did not tell them what they wanted to hear. By this they debased not me but themsleves and their people, for they showed that the British police and the German Gestapo were on the same plane.

"I have not come to ask any favors of you. I merely want to tell you plainly that I do not recognize your right to judge me for two reasons: first, because you are officers of the British army and are in this country as occupying forces who have taken it over by military might. On the other hand, my connection with this country stems from a divine law, from millenia of history, from a right which has been recognized by 52 nations, from an eternal love, a striving for freedom, an age-old faith which defies description. It is because your rulers govern with an iron fist that they are able to maintain a regime of terror and absolute power. They can put us behind prison bars and keep us enchained. But they can not *judge* us. They will never be able to force us to believe that they are the judges and we the guilty ones, they the accusers and we the accused. For there is no judgment without law and the law of the iron fist is no law. In a regime that rules with the fist there are neither judges nor judged. There are only cruel oppressors on the one hand and the righteous oppressed on the other.

"The second reason why I do not recognize your right to judge me is the *Emergency Regulations*—I use this term in a technical sense only—by virtue of which you were appointed my judges. You call it 'Emergency Regulations' but the entire Jewish community and every freedom-loving person the world over views it as a system of anarchy unequalled in the history of any country, even that of the totalitarian ones. There is not a single person in Palestine, therefore, who recognizes the legality and moral worth of your system of law. Every sentence which is passed on the basis of it is considered by every Jew, without exception, an

act of irresponsibility, a breach of the fundamental rights
of every citizen.

"It goes without saying that I realize my protest will be
of no avail. You will probably continue with the agenda,
refer to the obnoxious pamphlet containing 'The Emergency Laws of the Palestine Government' and issue your
verdict on the basis of one or more of its paragraphs. It
may be that there were days—they seem to have been
so long ago, although in reality this is not so—when an
accused person such as myself—I use the term in a technical
sense only—could convince his judges or at least one of
his judges, of his righteousness and the justice of his cause.
In those days Emil Zola stood up against his own people and
rulers and championed a Jew or, better still, the ideal of
justice which this Jew represented. In those days Byron
sacrificed his life in the battle of a small oppressed nation
for liberation. In those days ideals, lofty strivings and
just ideas had value even in your country. But those days
are gone; a new generation has arisen which relies on
hypocrisy rather than understanding, on cruelty rather than
intelligence. It is a generation of people with narrow minds
and closed hearts, a generation not of Zolas, Byrons and
Wedgewoods but of small people who have taken over
high positions and demand honesty of others while they
themselves are prepared to cheat and pervert and to practice cruelty, oppression and exploitation. One cannot expect that such a generation should revolt against its leaders
who besmirch its name and bring down upon it eternal
shame. During such a generation there is not a single
person to arise and proclaim: we have sinned against the
Jewish people, we have betrayed it, we had a share in
the extermination of millions of its sons and children, we
have criminally taken the land which the Almighty gave
them as an eternal inheritance and whose rebuilding we
ourselves promised to aid. We have sinned and must correct
our mistakes. The Jews who sacrifice their lives so that
their persecuted brethren might return to their land and
live in freedom deserve honor and respect and we ought
to bow our heads to them. No! Such an honest and
courageous voice was not lifted in your country because

there was simply no one to do it. This is the curse of a generation that builds military bases on an ocean of blood, on millions of dead, on the grave of an eternal hope, on the brink of flaming hatred. I thereore harbor no illusions that I can convince you to put your conscience before your careers. I do not personally blame you for being sent here. You were given orders to issue a verdict and probably will carry them out.

"But before you do so I want you to hear a few words of warning from a son of a people whose existence is proof that tyranny and wickedness cannot prevail.

"The ancient Romans had a proverb: 'Woe to the conquered.' Who knows this better than we Jews who have undergone so much suffering and so many trials from the time of the struggle between tiny Judea and the mighty Roman Empire to this day. But you, gentlemen, will prove to the world that the converse of the Latin proverb is also true: 'Woe to the conqueror.'

"You have just celebrated the anniversary of your victory over Nazi Germany, but have you really been victorious? True, with the aid of two powerful allies you have physically broken the enemy, but woe to such a victory when the spirit of the enemy has conquered you. You know very well that it has conquered you. For were it not so, how could you treat the people that was the first victim of Nazism as you do? How could you collaborate with those who undertook the mass extermination of the Jewish people? How could you shut in the face of the children of this people the gates of their homeland, the only chance of salvation? How could you keep them in concentration camps and gloat over the fact? How could you rob them of their last hope? How could you sentence an entire people to destruction only because you wanted to appropriate its country for your own sinister, nefarious motives? And at times it seemed to you that you would achieve these horrible aims by putting an end to our people's striving for life and freedom. No, gentlemen, all this would have been unlikely had you not drunk from the poisoned cup of eternal hatred held out by Hitler, his teachings and disciples. You have drunk from this cup to the

point of drunkenness and therefore have rendered yourselves
an obstacle in the path of a people that is returning to its
age-old home after having suffered so much in the *galut*.
You have stood in the way and said: no, you cannot pass;
you cannot go to Zion, only to destruction.

"If so, gentlemen, if you have been tainted by the spirit
of Nazism, if you have assumed the role of *Pharaoh,
Amalek, Nebuchadnezzer* and *Antiochus,* of *Haman* and
Hitler, bethink yourselves and look at the fiery inscription
on the wall which no one can erase. With such a spirit and
such a program you cannot hope to exist either as an empire or a nation. No military bases will save you and no
physical power will extricate you from your precarious
position. A greater power than you will arise to destroy
you. True, until that time you shall be able to visit more
troubles upon our people, you shall still spill our blood and
kill many of our children. But you shall not be able to
destroy us. Each time we will arise anew and defend the
existence of our people, the eternal people. We will fight
for the land because it is ours. You will not annihilate us.
We appeared on the scene of history long before you and
will remain long after you. You had better take care, for
God's justice will surely not bypass you."

THE DEATH SENTENCE

On the following day, June 13, the "court" pronounced the
death "sentence" on both *Irgun* fighters. The British officer-
"judges," or more exactly, the British military staff which
dictated the "sentence," could not forgive its humiliating defeat
and sought to wipe it away with revenge.

The defendants received their "sentence" courageously and
calmly. From the death cell, Ashbel wrote the following to a
friend:

"It has occurred to me that not once during the two
days I have been in the death cell, I thought about the fate
which awaits me. Do you think that I have lost all feeling,

that I do not realize what is ahead of me?. But my calm
is a result of psychological preparation throughout the
years, of the readiness to lay down one's life for the homeland expressed in our children's songs and the realities of
life. Yes! I realize what awaits me, but I am certain that
my death will bring us a step nearer to success. It matters
not! With our blood, our deaths and our sacrifices we will
erect a free state for our people who will know how to
live and will have something to live for.

" 'Only by blood can a country be redeemed,
Only a country redeemed by blood
Is sanctified for its people with the sanctity of blood.' "
(From a poem by *Uri Zvi Greenberg*)

The reaction of the Jewish masses to the "sentence," however, was one of deep concern. The majority of Jews had strong
sympathy for the *Irgun* cause throughout the revolt. As pointed
out, this was the period during which the *Haganah* had joined
in the fighting. *Davar,* the organ of the *Histadrut,* tried to
condemn the arms confiscation but its own readers and sympa-
thizers could not understand why it should be permissible for
the *Haganah* to blow up bridges and yet be wrong for the *Irgun*
to confiscate arms. . . . The *Haganah* members well understood
that the death "sentence" could lead to quite serious results and
to a break in the agreement between the Jewish forces. The
entire *Yishuv* and its press therefore appealed to General Barker,
Commander-in-Chief of the British army in Palestine and to
General Cunningham, the High Commissioner, to substitute
another "punishment" for the death "sentence."

ARREST FOR ARREST

The *Irgun,* however, was cognizant of the true value of this
appeal. The relations between the Jewish Agency and the
British administration had been strained since November, 1945.

This was not due to the participation of the *Haganah* in the struggle. What the British regretted was that the *Haganah* had ceased its practice of handing over lists of those suspected of being Irgunists. It was quite possible therefore, that a general appeal to commute the death "sentence" would meet with British opposition. For this reason the *Irgun* decided to stop the British from murdering the two *Irgun* soldiers. On June 18, four days after the "sentence" had been made known, a well-trained group of *Irgun* soldiers disguised as British officers entered the large, sumptuous Yarkon Hotel on Yarkon Street in Tel Aviv, which served as a gathering-place for British officers. Under threat of arms, they forced five British officers to accompany them and quickly left, before the remaining frightened officers had the courage to call for help.

In Jerusalem, too, a group of *Irgun* soldiers arrested a British officer. It later became known that he was Major H. B. Chadwick, a member of the highest military headquarters in Palestine. In Tel Aviv the arrestees were Air Force Lieut. Russel, and Captains Spencer, Ray, Wharton and Taylor. Such a reaction was entirely unexpected by the British. This was the first time that Britons had been arrested by the *Irgun* and this fact alone greatly perturbed them.

That same afternoon, the military commander of the Lydda-Tel Aviv district informed the Mayor of Tel Aviv that if the British officers were not freed by the next morning, he would place the city under strict "curfew" and carry out careful searches. He also hinted that the British would not be over-careful during the searches. This was a clear indication that the army would be given a free hand to start pogroms. This warning caused a panic in the Municipal Council called into special session by the Mayor.

Early that evening, Israel Rokach, the Mayor of Tel Aviv, called upon me to transmit to the *Irgun* the British demand for the freeing of the officers. He added that he would make every effort to procure a pardon for the *Irgun* soldiers and requested that the British officers be freed that very evening, before the proclamation of the "curfew." An hour later I gave him the official reply of the *Irgun*: the *Irgun* was unprepared to enter into any negotiations with the British administration. This was a struggle between two military forces and as long as the British refused to grant that an imprisoned soldier could not be brought to trial, and particularly that he could not be sentenced, there could be no talk about freeing the British arrestees. I explained also that if the British would dare start pogroms against the peaceful population, they would pay with their lives for it.

That same night a strict "curfew" was proclaimed over Tel Aviv and the surrounding settlements. The "curfew" applied also to all roads leading to and from the city. Thousands of soldiers occupied Tel Aviv. The entire economic life of the area was at a standstill. Before twenty-four hours had passed and even before the soldiers had begun their searches, the Government had to call off the "curfew." It remained in force only on the roads.

This happened because the two Jews on whom the British High Commissioner had counted upon to help obtain the release of the British arrestees without meeting the *Irgun* demand, could do nothing. The first was Dr. Chaim Weizmann who was called to see the High Commissioner during the early hours of the "curfew." The latter heard Dr. Weizmann clearly say that he had no influence over the *Irgun* and could not enter into the affair. The second was Mr. Rokach. He also stated that he had no influence over the *Irgun* but he advised the High Commissioner to lift the "curfew," so that he could make an effort to get in touch with people who knew how to reach the *Irgun*. At the same time. he cautiously gave the High Commissioner to understand that the "verdict" against the two *Irgun* soldiers would have to be commuted. Regarding the first "suggestion," the High Commissioner agreed immediately. Regarding the second he stated that he was also of the same opinion and that having been in touch with London about it he was now awaiting confirmation of his view.

A FEW ARE FREED

During this time Major Chadwick himself "negotiated" with the *Irgun* people who had him under arrest. He swore that as an officer of the highest military staff he would endeavor to persuade General Barker to revoke the "verdict" against Ashbel and Simchon. The *Irgun* decided to free him. It was also decided to liberate two other arrestees in Tel Aviv. After Rokach had communicated the results of his conversation with the High Commissioner, it was clear to the *Irgun* that the "verdict" would be revoked and it was considered enough to keep three officers under arrest.

All these events on the outside had no effect on the "sentenced" *Irgun* men. With calm and dignity they sat in their death cells and waited. . . . This is what Ashbel wrote to his friend during those days:

> "I await my hanging with a feeling of assurance that I have not disappointed my officers. Although my red blouse does not bear the symbol of the *Irgun,* I have completely fulfilled my oath."

Only two days after the conversation between the High Commissioner and Mr. Rokach, the British began to hope anew that they would secure the freedom of their arrested officers without having to meet the *Irgun* demand. . . . Again it was a Jewish party that intervened. . . . The combined *Tnuat Hameri* (Resistance Movement) was then functioning and it unified the various fighting groups. The *Haganah* tried to use its majority to force the *Irgun* to free the British arrestees without any conditions. It promised that if after the freeing of the arrestees. the British would hang the two *Irgun* soldiers, British blood would be spilled in the street. When Ashbel found out about this he wrote :

"If our death can become a basis for unity in the struggle of the entire *Yishuv,* we are prepared to forego the pardon which might be granted us. Who knows better than we what a force this united struggle could become. . . ."

The *Irgun* was uncertain, however, whether the *Haganah,* or more exactly the Jewish Agency which controlled the *Haganah,* would keep its word, the more so because of previous sad experiences in counting on promises of the *Haganah.* The lives of two of its faithful and heroic soldiers were at stake. It therefore rejected the demand of the *Haganah* to free the British arrestees. But the *Haganah's* move in itself was grounds enough for the British to hope they could obtain the release of their officers without repayment and then . . . hang the two *Irgun* soldiers.

During the absorbing days of the fight for the lives of Ashbel and Simchon there emerged a new factor through which the British hoped to destroy the unity of the Resistance Movement. On June 29 a number of members of the Jewish Agency and the *Vaad Leumi* were placed under arrest. The Jewish Agency building was occupied by British soldiers and investigations were conducted in many *Kibbutzim.* Ostensibly, the British searched for "illegal immigrants," but at the same time they despoiled and destroyed everything that fell into their hands. In Yagur, a kibbutz near Haifa, there occurred a virtual pogrom and its buildings were destroyed because arms were discovered there, arms of which the British had been well aware previously. . . . Thousands of kibbutz members were arrested and brought to a new concentration camp—Rafiah (Rafa), near the Egyptian border. The British claimed to be searching for "illegal immigrants" but it was no secret that they were trying to destroy the unity of the Resistance Movement by demonstrating to the *Haganah* that if they would not break with the *Irgun* and Stern Group, the British would consider them also as "terrorists" and treat them in the same fashion as the others. . . . The British tried to force the *Haganah* into renewing its collaboration with the police. They were sure that after the few months of joint activity, the *Haganah* knew all the secrets of the *Irgun* and that a deathblow could now be dealt that organization.

But the British were again mistaken. True, by their action of June 29, they weakened the *Haganah's* determination to fight. The *Haganah* was not so militant and after its first serious clash with the British, it withdrew from the struggle. But their main plan of breaking the *Irgun* by means of the *Haganah* fell through. As pointed out, even during the months of unity the *Irgun* succeeded in maintaining its sercrets, so that the *Haganah* knew little even then about its activities.

THE IRGUN TRIUMPHS

By July 3, the British had lost all hope of obtaining the release of the British arrestees with the aid of the *Haganah* and were forced to accept the *Irgun* demands. An official announcement over the Jerusalem radio stated that General Barker, Commander-in-Chief of the British forces in Palestine, had confirmed the death "sentence" over Ashbel and Simchon but that High Commissioner Cunningham had granted them amnesty. . . . After this declaration by the Government, it remained for the *Irgun* to release the British arrestees in a manner which would preclude discovery of their place of detention. The *Irgun* announced that the Britons would be freed as soon as the Government removed the "curfew" from the roads to Tel Aviv. On July 4, the Jerusalem radio announced the lifting of the road "curfew." An hour later a truck drew up on Rothschild Boulevard near the corner of Shadal Street in Tel Aviv, deposited a large wooden case and immediately disappeared. To the surprise of the passers-by the case began to move. . . . A number of people hurried to it and removed the cover. . . .

Out came three British officers. . . . They were Captains Spencer, Wharton and Taylor. They went immediately to the nearest police station and made their first statement: they did not know where they had been detained; they could not recognize those who held them because the latter had worn masks and any search for their captors would be futile; they had received good treatment. . . .

In fact the British prisoners had been so impressed by the treatment they received, that they insisted in conversations with their *Irgun* captors, prior to their release, that they would oppose any attempt to search for their abductors or the place of detention.

This statement naturally did not prevent the British police and soldiers from trying to find traces of the place of imprisonment or from coming to Latrun a few weeks later to search among the arrestees. They were unsuccessful, but again they demonstrated the value of a British promise. . . .

ON THE BARRICADES

By Michael Ashbel

(Translated from the Hebrew)

I

Today we part, little Sarah,
As I go to battle
For our State
On both sides of the Jordan.
Cut your braids,
Gird yourself well,
Embrace me, take a gun
And join me in the ranks.

On the barricades, on the barricades we'll meet.
On the barricades for freedom we'll fight,
Our gunbarrels side by side.
Our shots echoing each other.
On the barricades, on the barricades we'll meet.

II

And if on the gallows
My life for my people I give—
Weep not,
For this is my fate.
Wipe away your tears,
Press the gun to your heart
And choose another
From my troop . . .

On the barricades . . .

Honor Above Life

A LL I remember of my first meeting with Dov Gruner was a pair of piercing, blazing eyes. Even his name escaped me, and for several years I could not recall it. It may even be that I never knew his name at first, for our encounter was strange, indeed.

I was returning in the early hours of the morning from a meeting. The streets of Tel Aviv were plunged in darkness made even thicker by a heavy fog. I was tired and dizzy from the drawn-out heated debates. We had discussed whether the followers of Jabotinsky should enroll in the British army without a solemn promise from Britain to support the Jewish National cause. This was a matter of life and death to many of us individually and to all collectively. I was walking slowly. The sound of quick, nervous footsteps made me turn around instinctively. A young man clad in a khaki uniform caught up with me. I could not see his face clearly but his eyes were like burning candles glowing in the darkness.

Dov Gruner in the British Army

He muttered his name in a manner of introduction and immediately took up the earlier discussion. He had heard my arguments at the meeting but did not agree with me. I was too tired to argue, so I gave him some perfunctory reply. He shook his head in disapproval. "I heard you at the meeting. You have a point, but we who have volunteered and those who will follow us tomorrow believe that once we are in Europe with the British Army we shall be able to save many of our brethren from the Nazi hell. This alone is worth the sacrifice."

This was a new argument, indeed. None of the advocates of enlistment had brought it up at the meeting. But I was too tired and physically unable to think the matter out. I replied, "Good luck to you," and we shook hands in farewell.

This was in the spring of 1942, when we were still unaware of the catastrophe that had befallen European Jewry.

AFTER SERVING WITH THE BRITISH

Years passed before I learned the name of the man with the fiery eyes, years during which millions of our brothers in Europe were put to death. I met Gruner again three years later, this time in full daylight. It was a beautiful Winter day in Tel Aviv. On Rothschild Boulevard, someone hailed me. I turned around and saw a soldier in British uniform sitting on a bench. I did not recognize him at first, but when he began to speak, the voice I heard years before suddenly came to mind. I looked into his face seeking those eyes which had so impressed me during our first meeting, but they were no longer the same. Instead, a sad look greeted me. I felt embarrassed. I groped for words to start a conversation and couldn't find them. Then as if trying to throw off the bitterness and disappointment which were weighing him down, he unfolded to me the sad picture of his life in the preceding few years. He told me of his early days back in Hungary, how when he embarked for Palestine it was his hope that he would, in time, bring his family over. But the war put an end to his dream. The Nazi hordes overran one European country after another and the fate of the

Jews of Europe was sealed. During the dark months that followed, Gruner's hopes rose that somehow his family had escaped. When the British called for volunteers, he joined at once. He wanted to be nearer his people. Somehow he dreamed he would reach them and get them out of the Nazi hell. Something else was in the back of his mind, too. If great numbers of Jewish youth were to fight in the ranks of the British Army, then, when the war was over, Jews would finally get their independence in their own homeland—in Palestine.

He spent four years in the British Army. In Europe, he visited his home town but the members of his family were no longer there. He didn't even find their graves. When he and his buddies tried to help the few who had miraculously survived, the British quickly ordered them back to Palestine to be demobilized. *"The Moor has done his duty, the Moor may go."* Upon his return to Palestine, he found the gates of the country shut to Jews and its shores under strict guard. Small boats, having made the hazardous trip across the Mediterranean with the few who escaped the Nazi rampage, were being sent back by the British. The *Struma* and the *Patria,* with hundreds of refugees abroad, were mercilessly condemned to the bottom of the sea after being turned away from the shores of the Promised Land.

Gruner was bitter and disillusioned, and it would have been too cruel for me to remind him of our discussion three years before when I argued against joining the British armed forces. I asked him to come with me and have dinner at my home. At the table he somehow brightened up. My children listened with bated breath to his interesting stories about the Italian front, and two hours later, when we went down to the beach,

Gruner no longer spoke of the past. Instead, he haltingly began to talk about his plans for the future. He was no longer despondent. Again he spoke of "fighting" and "saving." That unforgettable spark in his eyes struck me again. When we parted I asked him, "What does all this mean?"

"I am going," he said. And I knew then that he was going underground to become an unknown soldier in the Army of Liberation.

DEFYING THE BRITISH

This was in the winter of 1946. The British oppressors had erected scores of fortresses throughout the country for their police and armed forces, as well as huge compounds and strongly fortified trenches. One of these fortresses stood at Ramat Gan near Tel Aviv, flanking the Tel Aviv-Haifa highway. It was a central supply depot for a number of smaller fortresses dotting the entire region, and contained a gigantic arsenal of equipment, arms and ammunition.

In the morning hours of April 23, 1946, when traffic on the highway was rather heavy, a group of British soldiers cordoned off the highway south and north of the fortress. All traffic was halted. This, in itself, was nothing unusual. Traffic stoppages and searches by the police and military were an almost daily occurrence in those times. The only unusual thing about this particular stoppage was that there were no searches at all. A heavy military truck drove up to the barbed wire fence. A young "British sergeant" jumped out, and as he showed the sentry a pass, the gate opened and the truck entered the fortress. It carried a group of "Arab prisoners" guarded by a few "British soldiers."

While this was going on, two groups of armed men stealthily moved towards the barbed wire enclosures and took up positions in the trenches around the fortress, aiming their machine guns at the courtyard and the building in the fortified compound.

Inside, the "British sergeant" was reporting to the Officer of the Day that he had brought in a group of Arabs who had been arrested in the vicinity and were to be held until some higher authority would decide on their disposal. A few policemen were called in to unshackle the prisoners and they proceeded to do it in good British tradition by administering a preliminary beating to the poor "Arabs." The "British policemen" who brought in the prisoners joined in the fun. But the moment the prisoners were unshackled they drew, from under their robes, tommy-guns and the "British policemen" who brought them in did likewise. The "British sergeant" then informed the Officer of the Day that he and his men had come in behalf of the *Irgun Zvai Leumi* to confiscate the arms stored in the fortress, warning him that at the first sign of attempted resistance he would be shot. The Officer of the Day and his men surrendered and were locked up in one of the cells of the fortress, after handing over the keys of the arsenal to the soldiers of the *Irgun* who started loading their loot on the truck. Everything ran smoothly until one of the Arab sentries, standing guard on the roof suddenly became suspicious and started firing his machine gun at the *Irgun* soldiers. The covering detachment hidden in the trenches fired back and silenced the machine gun. The truck, loaded to capacity, retreated at top speed. The entrenched *Irgun* soldiers covered the retreat, firing continuously.

Two of them fell in the ensuing battle. Police and British troops, alarmed by the firing, began streaming towards the fortress. Another minute's delay would have meant the total destruction of the covering detachment. To carry the casualties would have involved additional sacrifices. A split-second decision was taken to leave the casualties behind and retreat immediately. It was only after the British had affected a thorough search that they found Gruner seriously wounded with a tommy-gun in hand. In spite of his severe wounds, he resisted so stubbornly that it took three policemen to subdue him and yank the gun from him.

TAKEN PRISONER

Before the evening papers appeared relating the heroic exploit of the *Irgun* soldiers, who succeeded in confiscating a sizeable amount of arms in a heavily manned British fortress, an officer of the High Command of the *Irgun* ("Abraham") Chaim Landau, at present a member of the Israel Parliament (*Knesset*), sat in my house. He asked me to get in touch, at once, with one of the lawyers in Max Seligman's law firm and instruct him to take over the defense of the wounded *Irgun* soldier whom the British had taken prisoner. Later in the evening I conferred with Mr. Max Kritzman—at that time he was still an American citizen—a young lawyer and a devoted friend who worked with Mr. Seligman and was in charge of legal assistance to the soldiers of the Underground who fell into the hands of the British.

The Ramat Gan affair was very serious. There was danger that the British police would let the prisoner die of his wounds without medical assistance, or even finish him off to avenge the humiliating defeat they suffered at the hands of the *Irgun*. The intervention of a lawyer was urgently needed, but at the same time it was rendered difficult by a serious complication: there was a possibility that the prisoner might have used forged identity documents because he—Bela Gruner—was at that time still

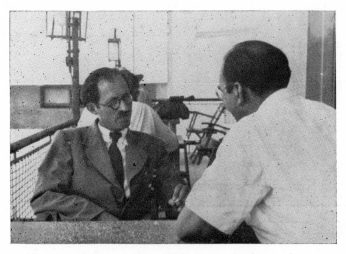

Menachem Beigin consulting chief attorney for Irgun prisoners, Max Seligman.

a British soldier on terminal leave pending his discharge. Kritzman had to be careful not to divulge his client's real identity and he proceeded cautiously, first to find out under what name Bela Gruner was taken prisoner, and then to take the necessary steps for his defense.

It turned out that all these precautions were unnecessary. That night Kritzman learned that Gruner didn't even try to hide his identity before he went into battle. The police found on him all his military identification documents, including his pay-book. This simplified matters considerably. But, at the same time, Kritzman experienced other difficulties in his attempt to see his client. The police were convinced that they held one of the high officers of the *Irgun* who had purposely joined the British Army to learn its methods, the better to be equipped to fight it later. This caused them to spare his life in order to exact from him information he might possess, but at the same time they denied his lawyer the right to see him before they could finish the interrogation; and nobody knew when the interrogation would begin as Gruner was severely wounded.

But Kritzman was not a man to take no for an answer. Also, he was under strong pressure from the *Irgun* to contact his client without delay. He knew that no *Irgun* soldier would answer any question of the police until a lawyer would come to see him with a prearranged password from the *Irgun*. And so a vicious circle ensued. Gruner wouldn't talk until he saw his lawyer and the police wouldn't let him see a lawyer until he answered their questions. Kritzman made an extraordinary effort to get to see Gruner and finally received permission to visit him at the prison hospital in Jerusalem. When I gave Mr. Kritzman the prearranged password, I asked him to consult Gruner on the line of defense which he would like to adopt. For this was a matter of principle and the High Command never tried, as already outlined in the chapter "Saved from the Gal-lows," to exert any influence on those who were to stand trial before the British. Kritzman therefore, had first to find out from Gruner how he wanted to plead.

I have known Kritzman for some years. During the fight of the *Irgun* against the British oppressor in Palestine I had occasion to meet him countless times. We once even shared "residence" in the notorious British concentration camp, Latrun. His home, as his office, was always open to anyone who came in behalf of the *Irgun*. On more than one occasion we spent nights discussing the defense of some prisoner. Even in the most serious situation he would have a word of comfort: "Everything will work out all right." But when he returned from his visit with Gruner he was agitated and visibly disturbed.

It was not the legal aspect of the situation that worried him. He himself told us that much time would elapse before a trial could be held. Gruner was seriously injured and the medical facilities at the prison hospital in Jerusalem were primitive. It was imperative to get a private doctor to take over. Machine gun bullets had shattered Gruner's jaw, and he suffered intolerable pain, particularly when he attempted to speak.

But what most impressed Kritzman on his visit with Gruner was his stubbornness and selfless idealism. Kritzman told me of the steps he took to get a private doctor for Gruner. He then gave me a few details of his visit.

One of the unbearable regulations of the prison was the prohibition on smoking. This doesn't mean that the prisoners didn't smoke. By all sorts of devious ways and means cigarettes were smuggled into the prison. Even the British and Arab guards supplied cigarettes to the prisoners at exorbitant prices which not all could afford. Gruner was the only Jew in the sick bay of the prison and he craved longingly for a cigarette. But when Kritzman tried secretly to leave some money with him, Gruner categorically refused to take it. "I know," he told Kritzman, "that this is *Irgun* money. Money that is destined to be converted into arms should not be wasted on cigarettes." Only when Kritzman promised him that he would deduct this money from his soldier's pay, which was due him from the British Government, did Gruner accept. "British money," he said with a smile, "may go up in smoke." He asked Kritzman that henceforth he should be called Dov Gruner, and not Bela Gruner. A soldier of the *Irgun* should have a Hebrew

Dov Gruner

name. Kritzman was very moved by this manifestation of courage, dignity and devotion.

The next day I went to Jerusalem and, with the help of some of the *Irgun* people there, succeeded in getting a famous doctor to visit Gruner daily in the prison hospital. It was not easy to get permission for the doctor's visits but after numerous interventions and the personal intercession of Chief Rabbi Dr. Herzog, permission was finally granted. The doctor, who according to reliable information, never had shown any sympathy for the *Irgun,* refused to accept payment for his treatment. He considered it a privilege and a sacred duty to alleviate the suffering of a Hebrew fighter.

The treatment was rather slow and several operations had to be performed on Gruner. By the end of the Summer of 1946, Mr. Kritzman began to think of preparing Gruner for the trial, and of discussing with him a line of defense. But, to our amazement, Gruner suddenly was transferred from the Jerusalem prison to the concentration camp of Latrun. It was without precedent in the history of British judicial procedure, that a man who was to stand trial, especially a man who was to be tried before a military tribunal, should be held in an internment camp where regulations were much milder than in a regular prison. This led many to believe that the British were trying to get out of bringing Gruner to trial.

There were good grounds for this belief. Dov Gruner had a distinguished service record in the British army. The officer under whom he served had great sympathy for him. In the Ramat Gan operation not a single Britisher was hurt. Gruner, himself, had been severely wounded and had passed through an arduous ordeal for several months.

Gruner also thought that his case was not too serious and when a plan was mentioned to get him out of Latrun, he categorically refused because he did not want to endanger the comrades, who would have to "make him disappear" from Latrun. "My case is not serious enough to warrant taking risks," he argued.

But all these hopes vanished when, one day in November, 1946, he was returned to the Jerusalem prison and a few days later, in December, was informed that he would be brought to trial before a military tribunal. Kritzman, who at once proceeded to Jerusalem to see Gruner, brought back a categorical and definite statement:

> *"I want to appear before the British hangmen who call themselves judges as a soldier of the Irgun, regardless of the consequences."*

The Irgun High Command accepted the decision.

BEFORE THE COURT

A few days later, Gruner's "trial" began. The British had an easy job. When Gruner was asked how he would plead, his counsel declared that he felt compelled to relinquish his duties as counsel for the defense because his client refused to comply with the regular procedure suggested by counsel. This, of course, was a declaration which Mr. Kritzman, a faithful and devoted friend of the Underground, had to make because otherwise he would have been taken straight from the courtroom to Latrun under the totalitarian Emergency Regulations of the British mandatory regime. Gruner himself simply declared that he would make a statement at the end of the proceedings. When all the "witnesses" for the prosecution, policemen and soldiers had finished "giving evidence," Gruner made the following declaration:

"Officers of the British Army, I wish to make a short statement: I do not recognize your right to judge me. This court has no lawful existence because it has been appointed by a regulation which itself is devoid of any legal basis. You have come to Eretz Israel by reason of an obligation which was entrusted to you by the nations of the world.

"You were entrusted with the task of correcting the greatest injustice ever inflicted upon any nation, the injustice of the dispersion of the people of Israel, which makes them the world's foremost victims of persecution and massacre. This obligation, and this only, is the legal and moral basis for your presence in this country. You have committed a wicked breach of this obligation, reduced it to a mere scrap of paper, and then tore it to pieces. Though you did not declare it openly, you acted exactly like the German Chancellor Bethman-Hollweg, who said: *'What is an international agreement—nothing but a scrap of paper. Is it worthwhile quarreling about it?'* Generally you have learned quite a lot from the Germans. Or perhaps on the contrary, the Germans learned from you. In any case, in one respect, their purpose and yours is identical: the purpose of exterminating my people.

"For you know only too well that the rape of our country and the closing of its gates mean a continuous mass attack on the lives of millions of men, women and children—my people. Notwithstanding this, or perhaps because of it, you are determined to transform this country into one of your military bases, one of many—and to steal it from the people which has no other home in the world than this, a home which was given to it by the Almighty and by history, a history sanctified by the blood of generations and a land which has been made to flourish by the blood and sweat of its devoted sons.

"After having cancelled and annulled the obligation which you solemnly undertook towards our people and our country you have no right whatsoever to be here. And if you are jurists, gentlemen, then you will certainly remember the classic legal principle: If the cause for which the law was enacted ceases, then the law itself ceases to exist. The cause for which the international law—under

which you came to administer this country—was created.
stands in contrast to the way in which you have corrupted
this sacred trust. It was for the revival of the Jewish
State in the country of our forefathers. Thus it is expressly
stated, even in the text of the League of Nations Mandate.
I say 'even' because I know, from a perusal of the documents, how you have endeavored (and you know how
to find ambiguous definitions which are open to conflicting
and contradictory interpretations) to define in well-balanced
words that Mandate, signed by fifty-two nations. In spite
of your endeavors, you failed to render ambiguous two
provisions which determine beyond any shadow of doubt
the nature of the obligations which you took upon yourselves.

"One provision recognizes the historical connection between the Jewish people and Eretz Israel; another provision
states that you were to undertake to reconstruct what existed in the past and was destroyed. And what existed in
the past in this country? Look into this book lying in front
of you, the Bible, and you will learn.

"But you mocked at, and in your arrogance, attempted
to trod upon the international treaty which you signed.
Therefore, nothing has remained of the legal basis of your
rule, and it is now predicated on one principle only: brute
force, bayonets, and a reign of terror in the guise of so-
called 'laws.' These 'laws' are drafted by the bearers of
bayonets; they promulgate them, they enforce them contrary
to the fundamental rights of man, contrary to the wishes
of the local population and international law.

"That is why I cannot recognize your competence to try
me. This rule, too, was laid down by the ancient Romans:
No one can transfer to another more rights than he possesses
himself. And if your whole rule is one of unlawful occupation, how can it confer upon you the power to try me, or
any other citizen, in this occupied country?

"A rule, existing in any country, when transformed into
a rule of oppression, ceases to be lawful; it is the right of
its citizens—moreover it is their duty—to fight against this
rule and overthrow it. This is what the Hebrew youth

is doing and this it will continue to do, until you evacuate this country and return it to its lawful owners—to the people of Israel. For this you must know; there is no force in the world that can break the link between the people of Israel and its one and only country. He, who attempts it shall have his hand severed and the curse of God shall be upon him forever."

Gruner spoke calmly and with dignity. More than once the usually phlegmatic British officers lost their tempers and tried to stop him. But Gruner was not a man to be interrupted. Undisturbed by the frequent heckling of the "judges," the accused who turned accuser, delivered his statement to the last word. Of course the "verdict" was fixed in advance, even before the trial began, and the entire proceeding was nothing but a sham. And so, on January 1, 1947, the pious puritans in His Majesty's service sent a Hebrew fighter to the gallows.

THE RED CLOTH

No sooner was the verdict made public than the *Irgun* High Command began considering the advisability of taking a few British officers prisoner and holding them as hostages until the death sentence would be commuted.

Verdicts of the "military court" were subject to review and confirmation by the Commanding Officer of the British armed forces in Palestine. And, even after confirmation by the Commanding Officer, an appeal could be made to the High Commissioner who had the final power of clemency. Some members of the *Irgun* High Command thought that action should be taken at once in order to force the Commanding Officer to commute the death sentence. There was a precedent for such action. During 1946, the *Irgun* seized large quantities of arms in an attack on the British military camp at Sarafand. Two soldiers of the *Irgun* were wounded in that action and taken prisoner by the British. They were brought before a military "court" and sentenced to death in June 1946. But in retaliation the *Irgun* seized British officers as hostages. All the efforts of the British to find the hostages failed. The High Commissioner was forced to commute the death sentence of Itzhak Ashbel and Yosef Simchon, on July 3, 1946 (see chapter on Ashbel and Simchon).

Some members of the *Irgun* High Command advocated a similar course in the case of Dov Gruner. There was, however, an opposing view. It was based on the assumption that the British were aware that even after the sentence had been confirmed by the High Commissioner, the Irgun could seize hostages, and that the Commanding Officer would therefore commute the death sentence in order to avoid the embarrassment of having this action forced upon him. On the contrary, seizure of hostages even before the confirmation of the sentence would make it a matter of prestige for the Commanding Officer and he might feel compelled to confirm the sentence in defiance of the *Irgun*. The *Irgun* was not interested in prestige in this case. It wanted only to save the life of Dov Gruner. Mr. Kritzman, Gruner's counsel, and a few officials employed by the British who were friends of the *Irgun,* held the same opinion. And so it was decided to wait.

The one man who remained calm and unconcerned all through this agitation was Gruner himself. Placidly he received the verdict, changed his prison garb to the red cloth worn by those who are doomed to die, moved into the death cell near the execution square and smiling, continued his consultations with his counsel. He was particularly eager to get in touch with his sister, Helen Friedman, in America. She, on her part, was trying to get permission to come to Palestine to see him and in the meantime, was enlisting aid in support of her brother.

The Hebrew press (save for the socialist publications), all the Jewish institutions (with the exception of the Jewish Agency and the *Vaad Leumi*, the National Council), initiated a series of interventions and demands to the Commanding Officer for commutation of the sentence. They told him the *Irgun* had issued a warning that the British would be made to pay with blood for the life of Gruner. The press and institutions were too well aware that the entire community faced a blood bath and their zealous efforts in behalf of Gruner were mainly motivated by fear of the consequences of the legalized murder cloaked in the guise of a "court sentence." But all these efforts were of no avail.

On January 23, Gruner was officially notified that the Commanding Officer had confirmed his sentence. Assuming that the confirmation had already been made public he didn't even trouble to let his comrades on the outside know about it. But, when he read in the newspapers the next day that the delegation which had visited a high government official several hours after Gruner had received the notification was assured that the sentence was not yet confirmed, he realized that the British were scheming quietly to lead him to the gallows without anybody knowing about it. He at once notified his comrades.

On January 26, the *Irgun* seized Major Collins in Jerusalem, and the next day Judge Wyndham in Tel Aviv. Leaders of the Jewish Agency and the Mayor of Tel Aviv were summoned before the High Commissioner who threatened them with severe retaliatory measures and martial law if the two Englishmen were not released at once. When the Mayor of Tel Aviv answered that owing to the curfew he could not contact anyone nor take any steps to have the two Englishmen released, the High Commissioner temporarily lifted the curfew. That same morning the Commanding Officer made public his decision confirming the sentence, adding that Gruner would have the right to appeal to the Privy Council (King's Council), which also acts as a Supreme Court of Appeals for the entire British Commonwealth. The Commanding Officer, General Barker, gave Gruner a few days in which to sign the appeal and promised that meanwhile no preparations would be made for carrying out the sentence.

CONSISTENT TO THE END

The declaration by General Barker was without precedent and this attempt to draw the Privy Council into the matter met with a mixed reception in the British Parliament. Mr. Churchill, while paying high tribute to Gruner's heroic idealism, accused Barker of having acted under pressure from the "terrorists."

Mr. Crossman, a Labor M.P., took the opposite view and while sharply attacking the "terrorists," warned the Government not to carry out the sentence but to commute it. The Jewish community in Palestine, over whom the death sentence hung like a Damocles sword, was partly relieved by General Barker's declaration.

But neither Gruner himself nor the *Irgun* High Command were swayed by this wave of optimism. In the first place, Gruner refused to sign an appeal. He instinctively felt that the British were playing a devilish game. It was not convenient for them to carry out the death sentence at this juncture and they were seeking time. This and more: they wanted to break Gruner's determination not to recognize the legality of the British rule over Palestine. By getting him to sign an appeal, they hoped to accomplish just that.

The *Irgun* High Command, unaware of Gruner's decision, evaluated the situation correctly and clearly saw through the double-faced game of the British. The High Command also realized that for the British it was a matter of prestige and as long as the life of a fighter was at stake the *Irgun* didn't care much about matters of prestige, the more so since at that time the *Irgun* had carried out an impressive number of military actions which were more damaging to the prestige of the British than any gesture of defiance in the Gruner case. The High Command therefore decided, following General Barker's declaration, to release the two British hostages, but in order to make it clear that the *Irgun* was not scared into action by Barker's threat of martial law, the release was timed to take place several hours after the expiration of Barker's "ultimatum." It shoud be noted that Barker didn't dare implement his threat, but even lifted the curfew several hours before the release of the hostages.

The so-called official Jewish institutions were the only ones who failed to see the realities of the situation. An immense pressure campaign aimed at persuading Gruner to sign an appeal got under way. In one instance a lawyer from Jerusalem who came to see Gruner in behalf of Chief Rabbi Dr. Herzog took it upon himself to pressure Gruner into signing the appeal by lying to him: he simply told Gruner that the *Irgun* ordered him to sign the appeal. Gruner, a man of truth himself, believed the lawyer and was ready to follow the alleged "order" of the *Irgun*. He only asked for one favor: to be permitted to formulate his appeal so that it shouldn't be confined to his sentence alone, but should encompass the entire field of "emergency regulations" in Palestine.

The next morning Gruner read in the newspapers a declaration of the *Irgun* High Command to the effect that every *Irgun* prisoner in the hands of the British was absolutely free to make his own decision and that under no circumstances would the High Command issue any orders regarding his course of action. Gruner, realizing that the Jerusalem lawyer had deceived him, asked Mr. Kritzman to come to see him together with the lawyer and declared categorically he would never sign any appeal or petition to any British authority or institution which, in his opinion, had no legal jurisdiction in Palestine.

The British, nevertheless, had won the first round in their war of nerves. The Jewish institutions, instead of pressuring the High Commissioner into commuting Gruner's sentence, directed all their efforts towards persuading the *Irgun* and Gruner to sign the appeal. Gruner was very annoyed with these unrelenting attempts. Strangely enough, the British authorities, usually very parsimonious in granting visiting permits to prisoners under sentence of death, showed themselves extremely liberal in facilitating visits to Gruner's death cell for anyone who might be counted upon to broach the subject of signing an appeal.

The *Irgun* High Command, too, was under constant pressure from various quarters. Chief Rabbi Dr. Herzog, the Mayor of Tel Aviv, Mr. Rokach, emissaries and official representatives of the Jewish Agency and the *Vaad Leumi* pressed insistently on the contact men of the *Irgun* to get the High Command to order Gruner to sign. They were told time and again by the *Irgun* representatives that Gruner and Gruner alone had the right to decide on this matter of life and death, but they stubbornly came back to the attack. Their attention was called to the inhumanity of placing Gruner in a situation which could break the strongest man, but even this didn't move them. All these go-betweens and intermediaries might have been well meaning dupes, sincerely concerned over the fate of Gruner and trying to save the *Yishuv* (the Jewish Community) from the bloody consequences which the execution of Gruner and the ensuing wave of retaliatory measures by the *Irgun* inevitably would cause. However, those who pulled the strings behind the scene and caused all this agitation had a different goal in sight. They figured that once they succeeded in having Gruner sign the appeal, the *Irgun* would be compelled to refrain from any large-scale action against the British so as not to jeopardize the chances of Gruner's appeal. And this was what they wanted above all. But the *Irgun* High Command and Gruner himself were not duped by this Machiavellian maneuver. On every occasion Gruner let it be known to the High Command that he would be very unhappy if the fight to save his life would deviate the High Command even for a single minute from the much more important business of driving the British out of Palestine; that he would consider himself a miserable failure if his life were to be purchased at the price of even the most insignificant concession to the British.

The British, meanwhile, continued their war of nerves against the *Yishuv*. On February 1, the High Commissioner ordered all the wives and children of British subjects and all the non-essential civilian officials to evacuate the country. The administration was to pay their transportation and the cost of their temporary settlement in any place of their choice outside Palestine. The Jewish Agency was informed that martial law would be declared all over the country. This created a new wave of hysteria and the pressure on the *Irgun* to order Gruner to sign was greatly intensified. The High Command sent a communication to Gruner informing him that he alone would have to decide whether or not to sign and that the *Irgun* High Command would accept his decision. Gruner replied at once: *"I shall not sign. I shall not recognize the authority of the British to try me and to pass judgment."* Only a few days later, it became clear that the *Irgun* and Gruner were right. On February 8, an appeal was submitted to the Privy Council, neither by Gruner himself, nor with his knowledge. An uncle of Gruner's, Mr. Frank Gruner of New York, was the signer. Had the British sincerely wanted an appeal they would have taken advantage of this opportunity. And yet, they rejected it. They rejected a second appeal. And thus, they showed their hand. They were only playing for time. Gruner had to wait three and a half months for the gallows.

THEY SHARE HIS FATE

In the meantime, the situation became even more complicated. During one of the military operations of the *Irgun*, six fighters were captured by the British. One of them Israel Kimchi, a minor, sixteen and a half years of age, was sentenced to a long prison term and to the barbaric punishment of eighteen strokes of the lash. The *Irgun* immediately issued a warning that if the flogging sentence were carried out, the *Irgun* would retaliate by publicly flogging British soldiers and officers. The British didn't take this warning seriously. In their limitless self-confidence they couldn't conceive that "natives" would dare to lift a hand against representatives of the "herrenvolk," the superior race of Albion. This writer saw a group of British officers in the colony of Hederah reading the *Irgun* warning (it was published both in Hebrew and English) and laughing very heartily.

On December 27, the British carried out the flogging of Israel Kimchi and two days later, on December 29, several detachments of the *Irgun* staged public floggings of British noncoms, and officers in the streets of several towns and villages. One detachment of five *Irgun* soldiers, driving a car on the highway between Petach Tikvah and Wilhelma, was stopped by a line of barbed wire which the British had drawn across the road. A skirmish ensued and the five *Irgun* soldiers were taken prisoner. In their car, the British found some weapons and a whip. The British, incensed by the humiliation of the floggings which were administered to their comrades, took it out on the five prisoners, whom they tortured and crippled to such an extent that one of the prisoners, Abraham Mizrachi, died of his wounds and the four others could not be brought to trial for several weeks. It was not until February 10th, that they were brought before a military court. Three of them, Dov Rosenbaum, (his real name was Yechiel Dresner, but this could not be disclosed because one of his brothers was an active member of the *Irgun*

רק כך

אזהרה!

חייל עברי, שנפל בשבי האויב, "נידון" ע"י "בית-דין" של
צבא הכבוש הבריטי למלקות.

אנו מזהירים את ממשלת הדכוי מפני הוצאה לפועל של
עונש משפיל זה.

אם הוא "יוצא אל הפועל, יוטל אותו עונש על
קציני הצבא הבריטי. כל אחד מהם יהיה עלול
ללקות 18 מלהות.

הארגון הצבאי הלאומי
בארץ-ישראל

כסלו תש"ו

WARNING!

A Hebrew soldier, taken prisoner by the enemy, was
sentenced by an illegal British Military "Court" to the
humiliating punishment of flogging.

We warn the occupation Government not to carry out
this punishment, wich is contrary to the laws of soldiers
honour. If it is put into effect — every officer of the British
occupation army in Eretz-Israel will be liable to be punished
in the same way: to get 18 whips.

HAIRGUN HAZVAI HALEUMI (N. M. O.)
b'Eretz-Israel

and held in a detention camp in Kenya), Mordecai Alkashi and Eliezer Kashani, were sentenced to death, and the fourth, Chaim Gubski, was sentenced to life imprisonment.   Gruner was to have three roommates in his death cell.

The prisoners did not defend themselves but chose to make the following declaration, which was delivered on their behalf by Dov Rosenbaum (Yehiel Dresner) :

Yechiel Dresner (Dov Rosenbaum)

"In behalf of myself, and in behalf of my friends, I declare that we do not recognize your authority to try us. We are Jewish soldiers fighting for the liberation of our country from your occupation rule, and since we have fallen into your hands we are prisoners of war, who may, by all accepted laws of warfare in the world—be placed in confinement but not arraigned for trial.

"We could stop this brief statement, and let you engage in your proceedings to your heart's desire. But the matter we are dealing with here is a peculiar one, and we do not exaggerate when we say that this is unprecedented in the history of our people and even in the history of your Empire. I shall therefore briefly elucidate the circumstances of our arrest, emphasizing that my statement is not to be interpreted as any participation in the proceedings of this illegal trial.

"We were stopped while on our way to carry out a mission assigned to us, which—to our great regret—it was not feasible to execute. We set out that night to protect the honor of our comrade soiled by your rule; we came to prove how mistaken was your assumption that only Englishmen are capable of a sense of honor, whilst we—the sons of the Jewish people—have no such feelings; we came to demonstrate that a new Jewish generation has arisen in this country which will not forbear humiliation, which will not acquiesce in enslavement, which will fight for its honor at any cost. In a word—we came on a mission of the National Military Organization to flog a British officer in reply to the flogging of a Jewish soldier who had been taken prisoner by you.

"We did not find that officer—despite all our efforts—and we fell into your hands. Nevertheless, we are not in the least depressed on this account. We are aware that our other comrades succeeded in carrying out their assignments and duly repaid you.

"This does not mean that we are eager to flog anybody. This does not mean we are glad to humiliate anybody's honor. Certainly not. We hold our honor dear, and we therefore respect the honor of others. But your approach is different.

"In the course of centuries you have become accustomed to bringing down the whip on the backs of scores of peoples whom you rule in your colonies and you thought we too would bow our heads to your tyranny. You were wrong. We shall break your whip, we shall put an end to the lawless maltreatment of those to whom this country belongs.

Now you know you are not going to flog the citizens of
this country, Jew or Arab, for we, the soldiers of Israel
have revolted against your rule and its debased methods.

"True, you contend that corporal punishment is still
applicable in your country. . . . This, in my humble
opinion, does not do you honor; but, after all, this is your
affair. You may flog in your own country; you may whip
your own sons to your heart's content. But off with the
brutal and barbaric hand from the sons of other peoples.
They want neither your favor nor your whip. Go into
your own country. Take your whips and your mediaeval
customs and return with your suffering troops to your

Eliezer Kashani

homeland. You will have peace then, and there will be
peace for our people, and peace for this land and all its
citizens groaning under the yoke of British enslavement."

One of the prisoners, Mordecai Alkashi, added the following remarks concerning their maltreatment under arrest:

"British officers:

"I join in the statement of my friend,, but I wish to add a few words about the treatment given by the soldiers of 'enlightened' Britain to Jewish prisoners of war.

"I would like the whole world to know that simultaneously with the denazification of Nazi Germany—so far as it is being carried out—there is on foot an evergrowing and intensified process of the nazification of Britain and her troops. Here are the tangible proofs:

Mordecai Alkashi

"After our arrest on the road near Lydda, one of our comrades who was not seriously wounded, died in mysterious circumstances following his transfer for treatment at the

hands of British troops. We were led under a hail of
blows to one of your military camps; we were immediately taken to an isolated room and British soldiers began
to tear off our clothes—not with their hands but with
razor blades. The clothes were torn, and with them
the skin was torn off our flesh. Blows with rifle butts
were dealt to our heads and bodies. We were bleeding
all over, but your soldiers were not content with that. We
were immdeiately taken outside naked and made to run
around the camp to the triumphant shouts of other soldiers.
Our legs gave way and we fell. They lifted us up and made
us run again and beat us again. Then they took us to the
room. We were given no clothes. They gave a blanket to
each of us. At few minute intervals, one of the sadists would
come in and remove the blankets from our naked, trembling,
wounded bodies. In the morning the torture continued. They
forced us to kiss the floor, they plucked the hair from our
heads and ordered us to sweep the room with them. Three
times they threw dirty water on our heads and made us run
naked around the camp. Then they began taking care of our
health. We were brought to a military doctor. He examined
us and asked the soldiers, 'Do you want to play with them
some more?' Of course they wanted to and again we were
taken by order of that doctor—the colleague of the notorious
doctors of Bergen-Belsen—to the camp, and again the beat-
ings, torture and humiliation were repeated.

"This, British officers,, is your countenance! This is the
dormant beast awakening in the defenders of your Empire.
This is how you treat captives. Is it surprising, then, that we
conceive not a feeling of disgust for you but an ever-growing
certainty that it will be your fate to descend from the stage
just as Adolf Hitler did? An army that can do such things
as were done to us, is not an army. It is a low gang devoid
of human feeling and human dignity, endangering the foun-
dations of life and civilized mankind.

"We have resolved to cleanse the Holy Land of this Nazi
scum and we shall hold no sacrifice too dear in implementing
this historic task imposed upon us not only by our freedom-
loving people but by the whole of progressive humanity."

'SENTENCED' TO THE GALLOWS

On February 13, General Barker left Palestine in great secrecy. General MacMillan took his place as Commanding Officer. It was hoped that the new Commanding Officer would not start his career by confirming the three death sentences, but soon it became known that Barker had confirmed the sentences just one hour before his departure. MacMillan could do no more than declare that the sentences would not be carried out pending the decision of the Privy Council in the case of Dov Gruner.

The war of nerves meanwhile grew in intensity. On March 3, martial law was declared throughout Palestine. All communication between cities and villages was stopped. Inside cities and villages the use of motor cars or any other conveyance was prohibited. A curfew was clamped down on the entire country. The British administration knew exactly what the decision of the Privy Council would be and it tried to hamper the *Irgun* and prevent it from preparing retaliatory actions even before the decision became known. The Jewish official institutions launched a tremendous pressure campaign and issued threats against the *Irgun*. They would use all their influence with the British to have the death sentences commuted they promised, if the *Irgun* proclaimed an armistice. As time passed, the effects of martial law became unbearable. Unemployment, the complete stoppage of commerce and industry and the growing scarcity of food owing to lack of transportation had a devastating effect upon the population—particularly in Tel Aviv, Jerusalem and Haifa where people had to subsist on starvation rations.

The *Irgun* High Command then decided to force the British to call off the martial law and lift the curfew. The *Irgun* began

a determined drive to halt all British military traffic on the roads
of Palestine. If the Jews were not permitted to move around
freely, the British, too, would be barred from the roads and
highways of the country.

One of many instances of the British reign of terror in Palestine.

Day in and day out, several times a day, British vehicles were
blown up as soon as they appeared on the road. Before martial
law was proclaimed there was always an interval between the
actions of the *Irgun,* but under martial law the military operations of the *Irgun* became almost continuous. The hazards of
traveling became so serious that British soldiers simply refused
to obey orders whenever they had to use a motor car or any
other conveyance on the road. The British High Command was
finally compelled to call off the martial law and on February 17,

it was officially cancelled. Again the British had to postpone the execution and again the Privy Council came to their rescue. While rejecting the appeal submitted by Gruner's uncle, the Privy Council deemed it advisable to state that "there is a precedent on record where another party has appealed in behalf of a person under sentence, but in that case the signatory of the appeal was the Jewish community and, therefore, the Privy Council had considered the appeal." This was a clear hint that a new appeal could be made. The High Command explained that after the failure of martial law, the High Commissioner would be compelled to commute the sentence and that any appeal to the Privy Council would just give him the time which he so eagerly sought. But all these arguments were of no avail. The official Jewish institutions seized the opportunity given them by the Privy Council and forced Mr. Rokach, the Mayor of Tel Aviv, to sign an appeal in behalf of the "citizen of Tel Aviv" Dov Gruner.

MORE CONDITIONS

In the meantime, the number of those awaiting execution in the death cell increased. In mid-March the British handed down a death sentence on a member of the *Fighters for Freedom of Israel,* Lohamei Herut Israel (Stern Group), Moshe Barazani, and in April two fighters of the *Irgun,* Meir Feinstein and Daniel Azulai, were sentenced to death for participation in the blowing up of the railroad depot of Jerusalem.

Meir Feinstein, like the others, refused to take part in the proceedings of the "trial" and delivered the following address in the British military "Court of Justice."

Moshe Barazani

Officers of the invading army: A regime based on gallows —this is your idea for the Holy Land, the land predestined to serve as the lighthouse for mankind. Your vileness and folly lead you to believe that through such a regime you'll succeed in breaking the spirit of our people. But, you'll soon realize your mistake; you'll discover that you are facing steel, steel that stood the test in the furnace of love and hatred: love for homeland and freedom and hatred against a subjugating invader.

Indeed, you are stricken by blindness. Are you really unaware whom you are going to encounter in this strife, which has no precedent in the history of nations? Do you really think that your gallows will affright us? Do you mean to scare us, who have for years been hearing the clickety-clack

Left to right, Daniel Azulai and Meir Feinstein being led in chains to "trial" before military "court."

of wheels carrying our brothers and parents and our finest people to the chambers of death. Us—who have been repeatedly asking ourselves, why did fate treat us differently than the millions of our brothers? How come that we did not share their days of fear and moments of agony?

To this we had only one reply: we have remained alive not in order to live and hope in thraldom and repression for a new Treblinka. We have remained alive in order to make certain that life, freedom and honor will be our lot and the

Meir Feinstein

lot of our nation and the lot of our generations unborn. We have remained alive in order to make impossible a recurrence of what happened there, and what is likely to happen under your rule of deceipt, your regime of blood.

We have learned our lesson, and paid for it dearly. But we have learned that there is a mode of life that is worse than death, and there is death that is a prerequisite to life. And, if you fail to see this vision of a nation that has nothing to lose but the irons of slavery, but the "hope" for a new Majdanek, — then you are indeed stricken by blindness and doomed by Providence to share the fate of all those who have lifted arms against the Eternal People. Assyria, Babylon, Athens, Rome, Spain and Germany have tried before you, and you too will share their grave.

This is what I wanted to tell you and your superiors, British officers. As for myself I have nothing to add to what has been said by my friends. I regard myself as a prisoner of war and expect to be treated as such.

The new Commanding Officer, MacMillan, confirmed the sentences of Meir Feinstein and Moshe Barazani, and commuted to life imprisonment the sentence of Daniel Azulai. The British Information officer, Stubbs, on making the decision public, explicitly stated that all the death sentences would be suspended until the Privy Council had acted on the new appeal.

The normal procedure in such cases was for the applicant first to appeal to the Supreme Court in Palestine and if that body refused to review the sentence, an appeal to the Privy Council could be made. On April 3, the British Supreme Court in Jerusalem rejected the appeal made by the city of Tel Aviv on the grounds that the Mayor of that city was not qualified to lodge an appeal because he represented a city in which lived not only Jews but also Arabs who were not interested in this appeal (Tel Aviv at that time had a population of 250,000 Jews and less than one hundred Arabs). This rather whimsical argument of the Supreme Court, however, did not teach the official Jewish institutions anything and zealously they proceeded with their appeal to the Privy Council.

REFUSE TO SUBMIT

All the efforts of the *Irgun* liaison officers to persuade public opinion and the official leadership that the British were just playing a hypocritical game and that their only purpose was to gain time was to no avail. Instead of trying to exert pressure on the British, the official institutions once more tried to pressure Gruner and his comrades into begging for a pardon from the British High Commissioner. Finally, the condemned sent an open letter from their death cell to the official leaders and all the go-betweens:

> If you cannot prevent the British from carrying out their scheme of legal murder, we beg of you at least to leave us, their prisoners, alone and let us die in peace and with a clear conscience. Stop pressuring us into asking favors of an authority which we do not recognize as legal in our country."

This letter finally put an end to all the attempts to get Gruner and his comrades "to sign." The following message was sent by the Commander of the *Irgun,* Menachem Beigin, to Dov Gruner:

> To Dov—
>
> We are sending you this message of brotherly blessing and salute from the depths of the fighting Underground and from the depths of our hearts. A multitude has risen to destroy you. This man Churchill, who is prepared to sacrifice millions of men, women and children (not his own people) in order to save the shattered British prestige, — demands your life. This British Government that calls itself "socialistic," wants your blood to be spilled for the very same purpose. British Lords and their Commissioners and the armies at their command that have challenged the existence of our nation, have risen against you.
>
> And you Dov, our brother, stand now, and for many weeks past, in solitary confinement and face THEM and death. They failed to bend you, these bloodthirsty rulers, for

they encountered a man, who had been dipped in the flooding rivers of Jewish blood, and rose from there unbreakable, nay, unbendable. Indeed, our brother, if there is a meaning to the word "hero," you stand for it, you spell it to enlighten and guide our children and children's children and our generations unborn.

Dov, our great brother! Your fighting family has done everything for your rescue from the hands of the hangman. Every one of us is ready to give his life in sacrifice for our just cause. This we regard to be our duty not only towards you, but towards any of our fighters that has been taken prisoner of war. Upon this we look as upon a principle of humanity which pronounces the life of a prisoner of war sanctum sanctorum.

Dov our brother, our brother, — the whole of the Hebrew youth together with all freedom-loving people throughout the world salute the greatness of your self-sacrifice and your outstanding valor.

On the eve of Passover, 1947, the commandant of the Jerusalem prison informed Chief Rabbi Dr. Herzog that the six prisoners in the death cell would not be permitted to celebrate the *Seder* (Passover Dinner) together with the other Jewish inmates. Dr. Herzog asked his private secretary, Rabbi Goldman, to find a Rabbi who would be willing to celebrate the Seder with the prisoners in the death cell. This was not an easy task because it had to be a Rabbi acceptable to the British and one willing to take upon himself this rather pathetic task of spending the Passover night in a death cell instead of with his own family. Late in the day, Rabbi Goldman found a Rabbi who agreed to go to the prison but added that at the same time he would try to add to this good deed another one, namely to persuade the prisoners to sign the petition for pardon. When Rabbi Goldman informed Chief Rabbi Dr. Herzog of the intention of his colleague, Rabbi Herzog asked Rabbi

Goldman to reject the offer and to go himself to the death cell for the *Seder*. At the same time Rabbi Herzog warned Rabbi Goldman not even to mention the matter of signing a petition to the prisoners.

The *Seder* in the death cell was celebrated with dignified gaiety. Were it not for the gray walls and barred windows one would have thought that this was an ordinary traditional *Seder* at which the old story of the liberation from Egypt was being told by people who did not have a care in this world. Only once, while Rabbi Goldman was explaining the meaning of the liberation from Egypt, Gruner remarked: *"It would be interesting to know whether the leaders of the Jewish Agency appreciate the real meaning of liberation."* But then he realized that he might have hurt the feelings of Rabbi Goldman, who was a loyal supporter of the Jewish Agency and he apologized to the Rabbi.

At first, it was very difficult to arrange the *Seder* in the death cell. Gruner and his comrades refused in principle to ask of the prison administration even a minor favor and there was no table, no wine and none of the other requisites for a proper celebration. But when the other Jewish prisoners learned that the inmates of the death cell would not celebrate the *Seder* together with them and that Rabbi Goldman was coming to conduct a special service in the death cell they arranged at once for all the necessities to be brought to those who were to celebrate their last *Seder*. Only once during the night did the stark and tragic reality of the celebrants come to light, when Gruner asked Rabbi Goldman, once more, to see to it that they be not bothered by all sorts of well-meaning people who counselled them to seek salvation in a petition to the British.

He pleaded: *"Let us go to the gallows with a clear conscience
and an unspoiled record."*

In all this turmoil there was one person, particularly, who
was unswayed by the general psychosis. Helen Friedman, Dov
Gruner's sister, never attempted to influence her brother to
sign any petition whatsoever. As an American citizen she did
her utmost to save her brother, the only survivor of her once

Dov Gruner's sister, Mrs. Helen Friedman, and attorney, Max Kritzman,
leaving office of Mayor Israel Rokach of Tel Aviv.

numerous family in Europe. She applied for a permit to go
to Palestine and asked the Jewish Agency in America to help
her get it. The Jewish Agency refused to help in any respect
the sister of the "terrorist" Gruner, but the British themselves,
in the hope that she might influence her brother to lodge an
appeal, granted her permission to go to Palestine to see him.

On February 13, 1947, Helen Friedman arrived in Palestine and was at once permitted to see her brother in his death cell. With the intuitive love of a sister, she felt at once that her brother was determined not to yield on this matter of principle which was sacred to him and she didn't even mention or hint by a single word the matter of an appeal. When the British realized that she wouldn't serve their purpose (the conversations with her brother took place in the presence of prison officials), they no longer were generous in granting her a permit for another visit with her brother.

The British, meanwhile, had succeeded in their immediate bid for gaining time. Public opinion was lulled into a sense of false security on the assumption that nothing would happen while the matter was *sub judice* in the Privy Council. Another factor which tended to take the case of Gruner and his comrades out of the center of public attention was the Passover holiday period when everyone was busy with preparations for the great festivities. This was precisely the juncture which the British were awaiting. Stealthily they began to prepare the gallows, without anybody noticing it. But the six doomed men in the cell could not be fooled. They knew what was afoot, and with great courage they began their preparations.

A FATEFUL PROPOSAL

On one of these fatal days, the *Irgun* High Command received a communication from Gruner on his own behalf and on behalf of his comrades. In it the six *Irgun* soldiers informed the High Command that they were not afraid to die, that they had made up their minds not to give the British the satisfaction

of hanging Jewish soldiers and that they therefore had decided
to take their lives at the moment when the British hangmen
would come to take them to the gallows. Their plan was to
blow themselves up together with their hangmen. This was a
scheme that required great courage and immense nobility of
soul, a scheme that could have been conceived only by men
who had long since resolved to throw away their lives if only
this could advance the liberation of their people. But the *Irgun*
High Command could not endorse such a plan lightheartedly.
An exchange of arguments began with the six prisoners. There
were many objections to their plan, the main one being that
suicide was a mortal sin in Jewish religious thinking. There
was also another consideration : should they carry out this plan,
their remains would be mingled with the remains of the British
hangmen and they might thus forfeit a burial in accordance
with Jewish law and tradition. But Gruner was not a man
to give up easily, especially on a matter of admissibility of suicide.
An outstanding rabbinical scholar of Jerusalem, whose name
must still remain secret, gave his opinion that in a case where
death was unavoidable, suicide was no longer a mortal sin.
Gruner then altered the plan and promised that the doomed men
would blow themselves up only at the very last moment and
that they would not die together with the British hangmen.
And so, both sides were secretly preparing; the British with
their gallows and Gruner and his comrades with explosives that
were smuggled into their death cell.

On April 14, Gruner, Dresner, Alkashi and Kashani were
suddenly transferred to the Acre fortress. Whether the British
did this out of fear of committing their fourfold legal murder
in a Jewish city whose population was in a mood of revolt and
where the *Irgun* had a strong following, or whether this move

was dictated by some other reason, the transfer to Acre created a panic in the *Yishuv*. From all quarters pressure was brought to bear on the High Commissioner to grant a pardon to the four men. But the British gentleman replied to all requests with typical British brazenness that he did not *"know of any preparations whatsoever for the carrying out of the sentence,"* and that as long as the matter was before the Privy Council no steps would be taken towards carrying out the sentence. The next day the Information Officer of the British administration in Palestine officially reiterated the same statement. That same day a group in Parliament asked the Secretary for the Colonies to halt the sentence *"if not for the sake of justice, at least for the sake of peace in the Holy Land."* But the Colonial Secretary too replied that the date of the executions had not yet been set. On April 15, Helen Friedman received a permit to visit her brother the following day. When Mr. Kritzman, Gruner's Counsel, telephoned the administration of the Acre fortress he was told that everything was normal and that he might come the next day to see his client.

Mr. Kritzman went immediately to Acre where he found Gruner and the others in very good spirits. They told him they were well aware that their end was near, and asked him to have Rabbi Arieh Levine see them before they were put to death. At this point a few words should be recorded in tribute to the outstanding figure of Rabbi Arieh Levine. With the greatest of devotion, disregarding his health and the weather, this beloved Rabbi could be seen on Saturdays and holidays, covering miles on foot, on his way to prisons to bring comfort and encouragement to his best children. How very characteristic it was of Rabbi Arieh Levine to ask, when 251 suspects were expelled from Palestine to the wilderness of Africa, that he be permitted

Rabbi Aryeh Levine, regarded as a father
to all imprisoned Underground fighters.

to join them. How very characteristic of him to say, coming to
visit the arrestees and detaineers, "I come to comfort you, and I
find comfort myself; I come to encourage you, and I find courage myself." He is one of the great living spirits that never
failed and never faltered, and no wonder that the last wish of
Gruner, Dresner, Alkashi and Kashani was to see him in their
last moments.

THE LAST NIGHT

In the early hours of the evening of April 15, a police
detachment came to the Savoy hotel where Helen Fried-

man was staying and asked her to accompany them to the fortress of Acre. Mrs. Friedman unsuspectingly followed them but on the way the convoy took a turn to the northeast and she was taken to Safed to attend her brother's funeral. At the same time that the police detachment came to take Helen Friedman *"to Acre to see her brother,"* a group of high British officers came to Gruner's death cell to inform him of the imminence of the execution. So jittery were the British that these pious puritans didn't even permit a Rabbi to give the doomed man the last comforts of religion before putting him to death. Gruner was unmoved and calmly refused to stand up while the "sentence" was read to him. On orders from their superiors two sergeants tried to force Gruner to his feet to comply with the British tradition that a doomed man must hear his sentence while standing. A fierce scuffle ensued and Gruner was battered and beaten a few minutes before walking to the gallows. This barbaric exploit was without precedent even in the bloody colonial history of "civilized England." During the burial in Safed, Gruner was clad only in shreds of his underwear, all battered and bloodstained. The Commander of the Acre fortress who, according to tradition, was to supervise the hanging, refused to do so after witnessing the gruesome scene in the death cell. He was immediately dismissed and his more obedient deputy was put in charge.

At half past two in the morning the Jewish prisoners in the fortress of Acre were awakened from their sleep by the powerful voice of Gruner who was marching to the gallows with the song of *Hatikvah* (the National Anthem) on his lips. Half an hour later they heard the voice of Dresner and at half hour intervals the voice of Kashani and lastly that of Alkashi; the fourfold murder was consummated.

The flag of Israel flying from the Tower of Acre Prison.

IN DEATH AS IN LIFE

On April 16, at six o'clock in the morning, some Jewish prisoners were summoned from their cells and ordered to put the bodies of the four murdered heroes into four previously prepared coffins and to carry them outside the walls of the fortress, where the burial society of Safed, summoned in the middle of the night, was waiting. At the same moment police and military detachments were roaming through the length and breadth of the country and proclaiming a strict curfew. Anyone seen outside his home was to be shot on sight. One hour later the Jerusalem radio broadcasted the official communique of the four murders in Acre.

Despite the strict control and thorough searches in the Acre fortress, the Jewish prisoners, who had been ordered to put the

The British hangmen watching over the funeral.

bodies of the murdered heroes in the coffin found on Gruner a letter addressed to the *Irgun* Commander, Menachem Beïgin:

"Sir:

"From the bottom of my heart I thank you for the great encouragement which you gave me through these fateful days. Be assured that whatever happens I shall not forget the teachings of pride, generosity and firmness. I shall know how to uphold my honor, the honor of a Jewish soldier and fighter.

"I could have written in high-sounding phrases something like the old Roman 'morituri te salutamus,' but at this moment it seems to me that phrases are cheap and skeptics might say: Anyhow he couldn't help it. And they might even be right. Of course I want to live, who does not. But what pains me now that the end is so near is mainly the awareness that I have not succeeded in achieving enough. I too could have said: *'let the future take care of the future.'* (Dr. Weizmann, when attacked at a Zionist Congress for his lack of vigorous opposition to British policies in Palestine, gave this answer—Editor's note) and meanwhile enjoy life and be contented with the job I was promised on my demobilization. I even could have left the country altogether for a safer life, in America, but this would not have satisfied me, neither as a Jew nor as a Zionist.

"There are many schools of thought as to how a Jew should choose his way in life. One way is that of the assimulationists, who have renounced their Jewishness. There is also another way, the way of those, who call themselves 'Zionists'—the way of negotiations and compromises. As if the existence of a nation were but another business transaction. They are not prepared for any sacrifice and therefore they have to make concessions and accept compromises. Perhaps this is a means of delaying the end but, in the final analysis, it leads to the ghetto. And let us not forget this: in the ghetto of Warsaw, too, there were five hundred thousand Jews.

"The only way that seems, to my mind, to be right is the way of the *Irgun Zvai Leumi*, the way of courage and daring without renouncing a single inch of our homeland. When political negotiations prove futile, one must be prepared to fight for our homeland and our freedom. Without them the very existence of our nation is jeopardized and fight we must with all possible means. This is the only way left to our people in their hour of decision: to stand on our rights, to be ready to fight even if for some of us this way leads to the gallows. For it is a law of history; that only with blood shall a country be redeemed.

"I am writing this while awaiting the hangman. A moment like this one is not given to lie and I swear that if I had to begin my life anew I would have chosen the same way I have gone until now, regardless of the personal consequences for myself.

Your faithful soldier, Dov."

Parents and relatives of the hanged heroes weeping at their graves.

UNITED IN DEATH

Less than a week passed after the fourfold murder of the heroes in the Acre fortress, and again the British were preparing to murder two Jewish fighters, Meir Feinstein and Moshe Barazani. On the night of April 23rd, they were to be marched to the gallows. In order to keep the hanging secret, the British decided this time not to transfer the doomed men to Acre. To avoid a repetition of the worldwide indignation caused by their failure to provide religious comfort to Gruner and his comrades before their execution, the British hastily called Rabbi Goldman in the dead of night to accompany them to the Jerusalem prison. While he inquired of them what was happening, he managed to say to his wife that she should give him the prayer book containing the prayer for Zion. She understood and, as soon as her husband had left the house, informed Chief Rabbi Herzog of the impending hangings.

When Rabbi Goldman entered the death cell, the doomed men knew what awaited them. After the religious service, they sat with the Rabbi and spent some time in conversation. They asked him to return home, and when he told them that he would spend all night in prison and would come to see them again, they insisted that he should not do so. Shortly before the Rabbi left, the two men asked him to smoke a cigarette with them and apparently at that time they managed to put away some matches.

A few minutes after Rabbi Goldman left the death cell and was seated in the waiting room of the prison a terrific explosion was heard. The entire prison was panic-stricken, for the guards thought at first that the building was being attacked from without. When the panic subsided, a thick column of smoke rose from the death cell and the British officers and soldiers who entered found the Underground fighters, Feinstein and Barazani, dead on the floor in a pool of blood. They had blown themselves up to foil the British hangmen.

The bomb which Gruner and his comrades had prepared for themselves and could not use because they were unexpectedly transferred to Acre, was put to use by Feinstein and Barazani

THE GALLOWS WAIT . . .

By Dror Gurion

The dark gallows wait in boredom and silently conjure up visions.
For nine years they were unsated, without revenge.
They heard not the song of life on the horrible path leading to a lonely death.
They viewed not the sure step, the proud, outstretched neck.

Now the forgotten vision lives again, past has become present.
They heard the song of hope, saw the upright walk and snapped the strong neck.
The gallows gloated over the feast of horrors. They rejoiced because they tasted blood.
Man created you—death-dealing instrument, and you will exact your revenge from him.

The dark gallows still wait; the bloody dance is not yet done.
Trembling victims still breathe in their cells; they are alive and await death.
They await the moment they will see you, gallows, as he who awaits his bride.
You too wait, rejoice and tremble. Yet you know not: their pride is their revenge.

What happened in that dark, dismal cell? What did it hear on that last night?
Did they sing, cry, offer prayers? No one will ever know.
No one will know the story of that night when death struggled with death.
A cruel death hastened the fate which awaited them on the morrow.

What happened that night in the dark cell that saw you cut short your lives?
Did the evildoers fear you in death as in life?
This only we know: when crimson dawn broke over age-old mountains.
It revealed the death of young lives that were born for the gallows.

The gallows stand silently and brood over their stolen prey.
They rage over the unheard Hebrew song, the outstretched necks.
The gallows stand. Casting their shadow, they see a vision of destruction and death.
Man created and sanctified you as an instrument of death, and you will exact your revenge from him.

April, 1947

British Rule on the Wane

(The hanging of Avshalom Habib, Meir Nakar and
Yaakov Weiss)

IN the Spring of 1947, the *Irgun* was already able to look
back with some degree of satisfaction on its past three and
a half years of revolt against the British occupying forces.
For at that time there were already evident on the political hori-
zon the first signs of British bankruptcy in the country. To some
extent one could already say of that period that it was the
beginning of the end.

The *Irgun* began its revolt in January 1944 with a force of
400 organized members. After three and a half years, it was
able to send thousands of fighters against the British, despite
the large numbers of its imprisoned, casualties and wounded.

The prestige of the Mandatory Power was undermined. But notwithstanding the success in the military field, things could not be left to take their own course and the *Irgun* could not rest upon its laurels. Further action was imperative. It had to give British prestige a powerful blow to shatter it completely.

That Spring saw the opening in the United Nations of debates over the Palestine problem. Bevin, who was forced to refer the problem to the UN after the first three years of *Irgun* revolt, wanted through international intrigue to get UN's consent to his remaining either directly or indirectly the ruler of Palestine. The intrigue was pursued along two lines: first, to draw out the debate in order that the UN should not arrive at any decision and that Bevin should be enabled to remain in the country. Second, to receive American help in the form of financial and military support in order to strengthen British rule in Palestine. The *Irgun* had to act quickly and on a large scale in order to make clear two things—that the Palestine problem could no longer wait for a solution and that the various powers should be wary of being dragged into an intrigue that could cost the lives of their citizens and soldiers.

No better spot for attacking British prestige and shattering it and thereby serving a warning upon other countries could be found than the Acre fortress. For centuries Acre had served as the symbol of rule in Palestine. Even victorious Napoleon could not destroy the fortress, despite the thousands of soldiers he lost in the attempt to storm its thick walls. The conqueror of Europe and Asia met here his first downfall. Also other armies were beaten back from the fortress' thick walls and moats.

The *Irgun* now concentrated on this fortress with the aim of delivering a death-blow to British prestige, of forestalling the new Bevin intrigues and of warning the UN not to draw out the Palestine deliberations. Certain British newspapers and high Palestinian officials later tried to interpret the breaching of the Acre fortress as an act of revenge on the part of the *Irgun* for the hanging of Gruner and his three friends. This was the interpretation especially of those officers who had advised the High Commissioner to grant amnesty to Gruner and his three friends. However, they were mistaken. It may be that subconsciously the hangings influenced the breaching of the fortress. But the operation itself had a political aim.

On May 4, 1947, while the UN was still undecided whether to permit the Jewish Agency representatives to appear before the Assembly or the Political Commission, or perhaps even only before the chairman of that Commission, on that day occurred the incident which electrified the world because of its daring.

IN THE LION'S JAWS

Under the command of the *Irgun* officer, Dov Cohen, a group of men dressed as British soldiers and officers rode into Acre in military jeeps and ostensibly busied themselves with repairing the telephone wires which surrounded the walls of the fortress. In the hustle and bustle of the coming in and going out of the Arab civilians and British on that warm evening, no one suspected that the group of men in military uniform and their "captain" were not British. . . . Unnoticed, the soldiers approached the municipal bath-house, "Hamam-al-Pasha," located near the walls of the fortress from whose roof it was possible to observe all that took place inside the fortress. A second group of *Irgun* men scattered through the surrounding streets and had

Dov Cohen, the hero of Acre.

the task of obstructing any attempt to pursue the attacking men after they had begun to withdraw. They mined the roads surrounding Acre.

When all was ready, the attacking group began to bombard the fortress from "Hamam-al-Pasha." One of the first two missiles succeeded in breaching one of the thickest walls. The group immediately raised a ladder and some of the men broke into the fortress and blasted open the iron gates that led to the cells. In order to heighten the panic, they set fire to the kitchen. The British police were so confused that when the Arab prisoners, who also had no idea what was going on, tried to seek protection in the British quarters, they were driven back with tear gas bombs by the British and had to flee the fortress. (Most of them naturally soon gave themselves up when the British declared that those who had fled would go unpunished).

The bombardment, the breaking into the fortress and the flight of the hundreds of prisoners took no longer than a quarter of an hour. Everything was timed. Every soldier had a task and the leader of the group, Dov Cohen, a skilfull soldier, executed everything according to plan. At the sound of the first explosion British military units began to rush to Acre but the road had already been mined and a military jeep was overturned injuring five Englishmen. The military units in the city were delayed by the *Irgun* men who engaged them in skirmishes and they were also unable to bring help. In this manner

Escaping through gate of Acre Prison.

Breach in Acre fortress wall caused by Irgun.

the road was kept clear for the withdrawal of the *Irgun* attacking group together with the *Irgun* and *Sternist* prisoners whom it had liberated. Despite this . . . an entirely unforseen coincidence hindered the withdrawal. That afternoon of May 4, there occurred the first *"hamsin"* (hot desert wind) of the Spring. A group of British soldiers from a neighboring camp was bathing in the sea not far from the fortress. A guard kept watch over their arms and clothes which they left on the shore. No sooner was the first explosion heard, when the group rushed out of the sea and ran fully armed to the fortress. It met up with the *Irgun* men and tried to block the way by firing upon them. Dov Cohen, the commander of the attacking group, had to put up an unexpected defense in which he himself, Shimshon Wilner Chaim Applebaum and Chaim Brenner fell dead, together with several others, among them Michael Ashbel (already mentioned above).

Shimon Amrani, who had been arrested after the blowing up of the quarters of the secret police in Jerusalem was wounded and ruthlessly murdered by the British. Chaim Brenner, mentioned above, had been arrested because he was found armed and later escaped. He was accidentally re-arrested later during a "curfew" but the police failed to recognize him. Merely suspecting him, the police sent him to Eritrea. A Jewish spy, who knew him, identified him before the police. Brenner was returned to Palestine, brought before a "court," sentenced to 15 years imprisonment and sent to Acre.

Hole blasted in wall of Acre fortress through which escape was effected.

THE HERO OF ACRE

Dov Cohen, the commander of the attack on Acre who fell in the battle, had an impressive record of military experience. Arriving in Palestine in 1938 at the age of 17 as an "illegal" immigrant, he immediately went to the Betar training center in Rosh Pinah. He came on a ship that was commanded by Eri Jabotinsky and brought by the *Irgun*. His arrival coincided with the day on which the British had brought the first Jew to the gallows, the previously mentioned Shlomo Ben Yosef. When World War II broke out, Dov Cohen volunteered for the British Army. He was sent to France and saw action at Dunkirk and Saint-Milo. Later he was transferred to Eritrea. There he joined a parachute unit which carried on its operations behind the Nazi lines near Derna. When the Jewish Brigade was established, he received permission to join it and became a member of the second battallion and of the same group (Daled) as Dov

British clear rubble caused by Irgun bombing of Acre prison.

British officer examining the broken bars
of Acre fortress.

Gruner. There he learned that his entire family had been ex-
terminated by the Nazis.

He was among the group of soldiers in the Brigade that
fought for the recognition of the Jewish flag and the Jewish
emblem. For this "conspiracy" he was "sentenced" together
with 30 other Brigade members to prison. After serving his
term, he was sent with the Brigade to the Italian front where
he was twice wounded and received British awards and medals.
After the Brigade was transferred to Western Europe, Dov
Cohen became one of the organizers of the "underground railroad," by which "illegals" were transported to Palestine. The
British naturally looked askance at his activity. He was demobilized and sent back with all his awards to Palestine, where he

threw himself into the work of the *Irgun* as an instructor in explosives. In civilian life, he was employed as an official of the Tel Aviv municipality.

Only under the direction of a man of first-class military training and underground experience could it have been possible to execute an operation such as the blowing up of a world famed fortress and to liberate so many arrestees. And all this by the light of day and under the nose of hundreds of British soldiers in the fortress, and in Acre itself. Were it not for the unfortunate coincidence which brought the British bathers on the scene, not a single life would have been lost except, of course, the lives of the prisoners whom the British heartlessly murdered after everything was over.

WORLD REACTON

The day following the Acre incident, Andre Gromyko, the Russian representative at the UN, stated in a speech.

> "Bloody incidents are taking place in Palestine. They are becoming more and more frequent. They therefore attract the attention of all the nations of the world and of the UN. They demonstrate that the mandatory system is bankrupt. It is because of them that the Palestine problem has been brought before the UN. . . ."

In a speech held in Edinburgh on May 6, Churchill said:

> "The prestige of England has been impaired in all parts of the world and her influence is waning with shattering swiftness. What a shame, and disgrace, when we consider that we have over 100,000 soldiers in Palestine. . . ."

The Palestine press was full of articles and descriptions of the heroic action. The following appeared in *Haboker,* despite British censorship:

"A number of factors are tied up with the Acre incident and it would be fatuous to try to overlook them. In the first place, the extraordinary heroism. It would be pointless to deny the value of liberating the imprisoned, an action which always has had a great effect on the imagination of the masses. It is simply unthinkable that it should not have the same effect in Palestine, particularly when the liberation of the imprisoned is tied up with the blowing up of an historic fortress which has been standing for centuries, which is outside of the Jewish area and which was breached close to "curfew" time (when all roads were occupied by the army). The Government was neither able to prevent the explosions nor the liberation of the imprisoned and it was unable to control the situation that had been created."

The English newspapers were also full of news of the bombardment of Acre. The *Daily Express* said:

"We must leave Palestine even before the resolution of the UN." The *Times* stated: "This is the severest blow which our prestige has suffered." The *Daily Telegraph* suggested an idea which shows lack of insight: "Without Jewish-Arab co-operation such a thing could not have occurred because the Jews of that area are opposed to acts of terror. . . ."

In the British House of Lords the Bevin-Atlee Government heard the following statement:

"This incident is without parallel in the colonial history of England, to attack undisturbed in broad daylight a fortress which was strictly guarded and in a country where there were 100,000 fully armed soldiers."

Such talk was heard also in the British House of Commons. It was therefore quite natural that in the ranks of the *Haganah* the incident should have had *"a great effect on the imagination,"* as *Haboker* put it. Dissatisfaction had long been voiced in the *Haganah* regarding the vacillating stand of its leadership which had quickly substituted a policy of collaboration with the British for co-operation with the *Irgun*. It now endeavored to minimize the impression made by the heroic act and pointed to the ruthless murder of the four prisoners by the British as evidence that it was an "irresponsible adventure. . . ."

The *Irgun* declared over its secret radio station:

"In broad daylight, in an Arab city, our soldiers attacked the ancient historic fortress which was guarded by hundreds of police and is located near the enemy's military camps. Our soldiers breached the fortress walls and liberated Underground fighters whom the enemy had held prisoner for many years. One of the newspapers called this action—'the greatest prison break in history.' When we consider the special dif-

Esther Raziel—First announcer of
the secret Irgun Radio.

ficulties of the action, this is not exaggerated. This was no 'suicide' operation, as maintained by our bureaucracy who blindly lead our people to destruction. This was an act of liberation which was carefully executed in all its details. Although the chances bordered on the impossible, a group of tried fighters who had been imprisoned in the fortress did succeed in returning with the attackers to their base. Use was made of the factor of surprise, of a strong attack and of covering the withdrawal by establishing full control over the city and its environs. All this was well planned and only an unforseen accident caused a number of deaths among the liberators and the liberated.

"The defeatists who pour salt on our wounds speculate with our blood and ask: 'Was it worthwhile? Look at the price you paid!' Cowards and opponents! When you blew up the *Azib* bridge and an entire *Palmach* unit was killed did we ask, 'Was it worthwhile?' When four men died on the barbed wire fences of Sarona in a 'terrorist act' we saluted them as befitting soldiers. We poured no salt on your wounds. We did not say to you: 'Look what a price you paid for your mistakes.' When Bracha Fuld fell and other soldiers of yours were taken prisoner by the enemy, we did not ask: 'What for?' And when you blew up the *'Patria'* and killed 220 Jews we did not blame you.

"For when a nation is fighting for its existence and free-dom—and there is now neither existence nor freedom—only cowards and traitors who give up their brothers to the hang-man will ask: 'Was it worthwhile?' Only chicken-hearted people who wait to be murdered by the hangman will ask: 'What for?' and only insensible people will say: 'The sacrifices were in vain.'

"Sacrifices in battle are never in vain. Only the sacrifices of the subjugated are useless. We offered millions of such sacrifices throughout the centuries because we were afraid to die for freedom and for life, because we entered the ghettos and failed to revolt while yet there was time. We had never learned to fight the battle of freedom.

"The Acre incident was an act of liberation, not an act of 'suicide.' It was not a mere demonstration nor an act of desperation on the part of those who had become tired of

imprisonment. Our members, Underground fighters, have
shown that they are prepared to suffer as well as to fight for
the homeland. For many years they sat and still sit in prisons
and concentration camps. They asked for no pity and guard
their personal and national pride. They suffer with dignity.
They know that their trials are an unavoidable part of the
struggle but that they are not at the end of the struggle. The
enemy is extremely cruel. Our suffering brings enjoyment to
his Nazi heart. He therefore does everything to increase our
suffering and that of our people. In this manner he wants to
force us to yield our homeland and to destroy us.

"We must therefore fight the devil. We must attack the
enemy with all the means at our command. We must make
his rule untenable in our country and render his life a hell
and his bases insecure; we must put his prestige to shame
throughout the world. This aim was effectively realized by
the Underground. A deathly fear has gripped the British
rulers. We shut them up in ghettos where they are insecure
and the whole world is saying: Britain is no longer capable
of ruling in Palestine.

"This struggle is our only hope. And the duty of every
imprisoned soldier is to try to escape and rejoin the fight. The
duty of his soldier colleagues is to come to his aid. Fighters
for freedom know of no bounds which cannot be broken in
the struggle for freedom. There are no prison walls which
cannot be breached where there is courage. Underground
soldiers escaped from the concentration camps of Sudan,
Eritrea and Latrun and from the Jerusalem prison. The
Acre fortress, which was considered impossible of capture,
we have shown to be no different from other fortresses. Yes!
We have again spilled our blood. But this was not the blood
of the slaughtered. It was the blood of fighters which brings
forth new heroes, generates courage, and assures freedom to
the homeland and a life of honor to its people.

"With sorrow for our dear fallen ones and with everlast-
ing remembrance we will continue the struggle despite in-
human suffering—the only way to life and freedom—until
the day when we will be able to return to Acre, whose walls
we breached today, and wipe from the face of the earth this
Bastille, this symbol of British tyrany. The day of liberation

for all the Zion captives is not distant. It will come as a result of the efforts of those who stand in the front ranks of the battle for liberation, who fructify the soil of the homeland with their life-blood."

CANDIDATES FOR THE GALLOWS

The reaction of the *Haganah* was not only an attempt to minimize the meaning of the attack but was also a clear indication to the Government that all the five men who had been arrested in the streets of Acre following the attack were *Irgun* soldiers and had participated in the fighting. The five were: 1) Ammon Michaelow, age 17; 2) Nachman Zitterbaum, age 17 (both were arrested at a distance from the fortress and at first the British had not known whether they had had any connection with the attack); 3) Avshalom Habib, age 20. The latter was born in Haifa. There he graduated from a secondary school and studied at the Hebrew University. For a few years he was a member of *Haganah*. When the *Haganah* began to vacillate and went as far as to collaborate with the British, he joined the *Irgun*. His parents, of course, did not know of this but because he loved them dearly he tried to prepare them for any eventuality. *"You must be prepared to see me with a noose around my neck,"* he once said to his mother. A few days before he went on the Acre fortress attack he said to her: *"I am ready even for death. I want you also to be prepared for the worst."* All this talk helped. His mother later sat in "court" and remained outwardly calm in her tragedy as she heard the death "sentence. . . ."

4) Meir Nakar, age 21, born in Jerusalem. His parents were from Iraq. When he was only 16, he secretly left school and vol-

unteered for the Jewish Brigade without revealing his true age. Upon his return from the army in 1946 he joined the *Irgun.* When his mother came to Acre to visit him for the first time he said to her: *"Be calm, mother. We shall yet laugh at the British; if not we, then our friends. . . ."*

5) The fifth arrestee, Yaakov Erma Weiss, age 23, had a more exciting past. He was born in Czechoslovakia in 1924. At the outbreak of World War II, he had already completed a Hebrew gymnasium (secondary school) in Munkascz and fled to Hungary with his parents. When Hungary joined with the Nazis and began to exterminate the Jews, young Erma, as a member of the Underground, had a special task to save as many Jews as possible. He somehow obtained documents from an Hungarian officer named Georgi Kotisch which enabled him to visit the various camps and remove groups of Jews on the excuse that they were to be tortured. When American airplanes began to bombard military buildings Erma, as an "officer," was the first to rush to "save" the buildings and thus he obtained hundreds of passports which enabled Jews to hide out. Later, his own mother and his large family were caught on the way to Aushwitz with their false passports. . . .

When the Russians occupied Hungary, his non-Jewish colleagues in the Underground offered him high positions in the new government. But the place where he lost his entire family and witnessed the murder of tens of thousands of Jews no longer held any attraction for him. He helped a surviving sister establish herself, and returned to his Underground activity, this time to organize "illegal" immigration together with the soldiers of the Jewish Brigade whom he had met. His own turn came to sail for Palestine on an "illegal" ship. The British apprehended the ship at sea and arrested all the immigrants, whom they brought

Yaakov Weiss and mother in Hungary during the period of
Nazi supremacy in that country.

to Atlit, a concentration camp for "illegals." The Resistance
Movement attacked the camp and freed 800 immigrants, among
whom was Yaakov (Erma) Weiss, who immediately went to
Nathanya and joined the local *Irgun* unit. It was a frequent
occurrence for people to embrace and kiss him in the streets.

These were the Jews whom he had rescued in Hungary, as well as those whom he had helped reach Palestine. But Weiss had to avoid such meetings. . . . He had already become active in the *Irgun*. . . .

On May 28, 1947, all the five were brought before a military "court." The first two, Amnon Michaelov and Nachman Zitterbaum, conducted their defense on the basis of being minors and also had legal counsel. The other three, Avshalom Habib, Meir Nakar and Yaakov Weiss, decided to do without their lawyer, Max Kritzman, and demanded that they be recognized as prisoners of war who did not have to stand trial. The demand, of course, was rejected by the British officers who called themselves "judges" and the three took no further part in the "court" proceedings. . . . Only when among the dozens of witnesses, Arabs, police and military men, there appeared the British soldier Locke and the British officer Hoffman did the "accused" inquire of the former:

> *"Why did you say when you took us into custody that the Nazi gas chambers in Europe were only child's play compared to what you would do to the Jews in Palestine". . .?*

Of the officer they asked:

> *"Why did you rob the money and watches which we had when you arrested us?"*

Both "witnesses" naturally denied everything but it was evident from the faces of the officer-"judges" that British honor had not been enhanced by such testimony. . . .

POLITICAL INTRIGUE

The defense attorney of the first two did everything possible: he cross-examined the witnesses, proved that their testimony was false etc. All this drew out the "trial." The officer-"judges" received orders to facilitate it as much as possible. Soon the reason for their haste was apparent. Bevin's intrigue in the UN had fallen through and it was decided to send a special UN Commission to include not only representatives of the Eastern bloc who, in their own interest, wanted to harm England, but also such friends of the Jews as Granados and Fabrigat. Moreover, the Commission had received wide powers, to which Bevin was opposed. With his usual boorishness, Bevin wished to show that he would not take cognizance of the Commission. The *Irgun* soldiers were to serve as the object lesson which Bevin would use to demonstrate to the entire world that he would ignore the Commission. The latter was due to arrive in Palestine on June 16 and Bevin demanded that the "trial" be completed by then. . . . It was therefore evident what the outcome would be. . . .

The *Irgun* decided not to wait for the "verdict." The experience of Gruner, Dresner, Alkashi and Kashani had been enough to prove that it was a mistake to wait for the last minute. The haste and impatience which the "judges" began to exhibit even toward the defense of the first two *Irgun* men clearly indicated what was to be expected. The *Irgun* decided to act at once. . . .

Between Tel Aviv and Ramat Gan there is a large swimming-pool called "Gallay-Gil." There British soldiers would come for recreation. On June 8, an *Irgun* unit entered the pool, which was brimming with civilians and soldiers, and without firing a shot forced two British soldiers to leave with them.

The British administration immediately began to adopt its well-tried methods. It called together the Mayors of Tel Aviv,

Ramat Gan and Petach Tikvah and threatened to impose martial law on the entire area. At the same time it offered to buy the aid of the *Haganah* in searching for the British soldiers. . . . A number of *Haganah* members from Birya had been imprisoned in Jerusalem because they were found carrying arms. They were quickly released. The *Haganah* allowed itself to be bought. . . . It mobilized all its strength and organized an extensive search in the area. It succeeded in finding the place where the Britons were being held and it could have freed them. But the British wanted not only their soldiers but also the *Irgun* men who held them. . . . The *Haganah* therefore put guards around the place and . . . informed the British general staff about it. Thousands of British soldiers began to surround the spot (between Tel Aviv and Herzlia) and to close in on it. The "operation" took a whole night and everything was done with the utmost secrecy in order to apprehend the *Irgun* men. But the *Irgun* had received knowledge of the route of march of the British and the *Haganah* and had ordered its soldiers to break through the British lines, even if it meant liberating the British captives. When day broke and the British were near the place, the two arrestees came to meet them. . . .

The *Haganah* still owed the British a "debt." It therefore kept its forces mobilized and prevented a number of attempts on the part of the *Irgun* to arrest other British soldiers. It meant that any attempt to arrest Englishmen could have led to civil war. This the *Irgun* wanted to avoid at all costs. . . .

THE HEROES SPEAK

In the meantime, the British officer-"judges" did everything to rush the "trial" to conclusion. By June 12 nothing further

remained but to hear the political declarations. Yaakov Weiss
was first. He stated:

"It is my duty to condemn your barbarous treatment of
wounded prisoners, which I witnessed with my own eyes.
Ashbel, Amrani, Brennen, Bando, Doar, Moskovitz, Schmuck-
ler and others were all shot in cold blood, although none of
them were armed. They were all among the freed prisoners
and none of them were among the attackers. I must say that
your soldiers are poor shots and that even at such close range
they did not succeed in killing these prisoners, who were
brought bleeding into the police station. There they were
thrown on the floor and left for hours unaided. Scores of
your human beasts stood watching them. All they did
was to prevent us from giving first aid to the wounded.

Yaakov Weiss

And thus Ashbel, Brenner, Bando, Amrani and Nissim Levy were left to die. I know that all these acts of barbarism will not surprise anyone. They will only serve to open the eyes of the people and to teach them the character of those, whom we are fighting. And other results will be achieved too. Until now we granted you all the privileges due to soldiers, in accordance with the laws and rules of warfare. In the future, we shall retaliate against you in kind and though we shall never stoop to torturing wounded prisoners and to your sadism, we shall make you pay for your crimes.

"Now as to what you call a 'trial.' We do not recognize your right to try us, free citizens of our Hebrew homeland, and we do not intend to participate in this mockery of the very principles of justice and civilization, 'the court.'

"Everything you do in this country is illegal: your rule, your courts, your laws which made our country the most abject police state that ever was and, indeed, your very presence here, against which the whole country has risen in revolt. This is our country from time immemorial and forever and ever. What are you British officers doing in our country anyway? Who made you the rulers of an ancient, civilized nation dedicated to freedom and sworn to liberty? Who made you judges over a people that gave mankind the very concepts of justice and law at a time when your ancestors lived in virgin forests?

"The days of your rule are numbered. The whole world knows it and you know it too. You will not be able to stay here much longer. Of course, you did everything a foreign oppressor might do in order to keep this country enslaved and to break the spirit of resistance of its citizens and rightful owners. You have assembled immense concentrations of armed forces. You have fenced off your barracks and offices with miles of barbed wire. You spent millions on police and informers. You looted, deported, tortured and to top it off, you murdered Hebrew prisoners and you brought to the gallows the flower of Hebrew youth. But what did you achieve? You did not break the spirit of the Hebrew resistance. On the contrary, you made it even stronger. The gallows which you erected in our country could not prop your crumbling em-

pire. And so your own Churchill has to shed tears over the fate of his beloved empire—despised and scorned the world over for the 'unholy war' it is waging in the Holy Land.

"The peoples of the world know that to establish 'military courts' in a foreign land, to appoint foreign officers, to threaten prisoners of war with murder constitutes use of force. The continuation of these conditions, inadmissible under any circumstances, becomes in the light of the UN resolution an act of defiance of all the nations of the world who adopted it.

"Therefore, from this place, where the will of the nations of the world has been so defiantly disowned, we turn to the United Nations, to the Special Committee on Palestine, and to all the independent nations who supported the resolution of Norway, and we request them to forbid the British oppressors to try us, free citizens of Hebrew Palestine, before an illegal 'military court,' and to murder Hebrew prisoners of war.

"As for ourselves, we know how all this is going to end. We know that our people will be free and that its oppressors will be forced to retreat in shame. We are calm and, more than that, we are happy. For there is no greater happiness for a man than to know with certainty that he will help to bring about the fulfillment of a lofty ideal.

"Hear ye, British officers, and tell it to your rulers who are stricken with blindness and do not see the handwriting on the wall: tell them that in this land a new generation was born to Israel, a generation which loves life but loves freedom more than life, a generation which will smash the Nazi-British tyranny, a generation which will achieve freedom even at the price of its life."

Weiss was followed by Meyer Nakar, who stated:

"As I stand here before you, it is my duty to ask what right you have to call yourself 'judges.' We know that you are not judges, but officers of a foreign army of occupation which has seized the land of another people and holds it in cruel oppression. Who sent you here? To this a clear answer was given in the General Assembly of the United Nations when a representative of a great power stated plainly:

Meir Nakar

'The British rule of Palestine has proved to be a complete failure.' The whole world knows that you are bankrupt in Palestine. A government whose officials are compelled to live in ghettos is not a government. A government which spends half the country's budget on its police and remains powerless against the people's revolt is not a government. One could cite at length many other proofs of your bankruptcy in Palestine. There is no force in the world that can save you from complete disintegration and final defeat. The members of your British Parliament contended a few months ago that there is one way to suppress the Hebrew revolt and that is to erect new gallows in the Holy Land to murder Jewish prisoners of war. You did that. You perpetrated one of the most hideous of crimes. But did you achieve your goal? Did you succeed in scaring somebody? Did you weaken

the will to freedom among our people? Did you crush the
national revolt? You know that you did not succeed. The
flames of rebellion are spreading within and without our
country. All you achieved is shame and scorn. No crime, no
matter how cruel or hideous, could save you from bankruptcy. And now the time has come for you to draw some
conclusions. A government that has failed in every respect and
in every field must go. The time has come for you British
invaders and bankrupts to leave this country, the country
which we shall build in peace and freedom and progress.

"Your rulers take offense when they are compared with
the Nazis. When Hebrew youth in New York paint a swastika on your flag, your newspapers are indignant and your
ambassadors lodge protests. But could you honestly say that
your flag can be cleansed of the swastika which you with
your own hands put on it. The swastika is the symbol of
oppression, mass murder, beastly cruelty, degeneracy and cor-
ruption. But above all, it is the symbol of the murder and
annihilation of the Hebrews. Whoever murders the rem-
nants of that ancient nation bears the swastika on his fore-
head like the mark of Cain, the father of all murderers. Did
you ever ask yourself, British officers, what task Britain is
fulfilling in this generation now that Hitler is gone? Didn't
Britain take over from him the swastika and all it stands
for? Isn't Britain in our day the only country engaged in
murdering Hebrews? Aren't British soldiers today murdering
Hebrews in Jerusalem and Famagusta, in Haifa and Kenya,
in Palestine and Europe? Isn't Britain holding tens of thousands of Hebrews in concentration camps? Isn't Britain plot-
ting to annihilate our people wherever it dwells? This is the
name you make for yourselves and this is a shame of which
you will never be cleansed. The swastika is glued onto your
flag with the blood of our brethren, the blood you spilled the
world over, the blood you continue to spill in this country
and elsewhere.

"A huge swastika hovers over Britain, just as the hatred
for which it stands dwells in its soul. You took upon yourself
a mission to complete the task which your guide and teacher
—the infamous Hitler—left unfulfilled. And therefore you

will go down in ignominious infamy the same as he went down. And you will fail the same as Hitler failed. The God who helped David to fell Goliath will help the bearers of the shield of David overcome the bearers of the swastika who befoul our Holy Land. Long live the Hebrew people! Long live the Hebrew homeland! Long live freedom!"

The third Irgun soldier, Avshalom Habib, stated:

"Before I go into the essence of the matter, I wish to say a few words about a problem important to me personally. After you failed through lack of brains and courage to prevent the blasting of the walls of Palestine's Bastille, a blind hazard helped you to achieve a great victory over some of the freed prisoners who were unarmed and over the three of us after we ran out of ammunition. Here your sadism and your inborn inferiority found full expression. Your men be-

Avshalom Habib

haved in the best Nazi tradition. They fired at the wounded; they deliberately withheld for several hours first aid from the injured and tortured everyone on whom they could lay their hands.

"I received a special treatment. I was threatened with murder. I was choked with ropes, noosed around my neck. I was cruelly beaten all over my body with particular attention to my sex organs and when I fainted, I received a drink consisting of urine mixed with dust and my own blood. I am not making any complaint. If I were to complain, it would not be to you. But the people of this world ought to know of the deeds of the British wild beasts in the Holy Land.

"I assume that you know the bloody history of your tyrannic rule in Ireland. You probably remember that there, too, you overran a small country and a civilized nation by force of arms and by treacherous perfidy under the foul pretext of protecting religion and maintaining law and order. You certainly remember that there, too, you exploited the working people to the marrow of their bones. You incited one section of the population against the other in order to maintain your domination. And when the sons of Ireland rose against you, when the Irish Underground waged a war of liberation, you tried to drown the rebellion against tyranny in streams of blood. You erected gallows, you murdered innocent people in the streets, you deported patriots into a God-forsaken wilderness; you tortured the people and looted their homes and you believed, in your stupidity, that by so doing you would break the spirit of resistance of the Irish people, that spirit which is a God-given gift to every man created in His image. You failed. The Irish rebellion went from strength to strength. The blood of the fighters and of the tortured united the whole nation around the flag of liberation until you were forced to retreat, leaving behind you a bloody trail and memories that will never be forgotten. Ireland rose to freedom and you were left with eternal shame.

"If you were not so stupid, you would have learned a lesson from history, you would have understood after what happened in Ireland only a generation ago and in America some hundred and seventy years ago, that you cannot subdue a free

people. You would have known that for every drop of blood
drawn by you, you would be held responsible before the
tribunal of mankind. In 1916, when your hangmen murdered
in cold blood four Irish prisoners of war, Bernard Shaw, the
Irishman who became a full-fledged Englishman said this:

" 'My own view is that the men who were shot in cold blood
after their capture or surrender were prisoners of war, and
that it was therefore entirely incorrect to slaughter them. The
relation of Ireland to Dublin Castle is, in this respect, precisely that of the Balkan states to Turkey, of Belgium or the
city of Lisle to the Kaiser, and of the United States to Great
Britain. . . . An Irishman resorting to arms to achieve the
independence of his country is doing only what Englishmen
will do if it be their misfortune to be invaded and conquered
by the Germans in the course of the present war. Further,
such an Irishman is as much in order morally as Britain is in
accepting the assistance of Russia in her war with the
Germans. These words uttered thirty years ago came true.
And if your rulers had given them some thought as we did,
they would have given up their futile attempts to subdue a
people through the gallows and bayonets. But you are blind
and no lessons will do you any good. Who knows, maybe
Providence punished you with blindness so that in the course
of time you will be made to pay for all the blood and tears
of our people both in our land and outside of it.

"Not only is history a closed book to you. You don't know
man's soul either. You think in your smugness that with a
given amount of well-equipped soldiers and with vile intrigues it is possible to dominate for any length of time a
country in revolt, a country all of whose inhabitants look
upon you as invaders, exploiters and oppressors. This is
another fatal mistake. Neither bayonets nor intrigues can
withstand for a long time the soul of men, the soul of free
citizens. For that soul is the pride of the Creator. It will
smash bayonets and void intrigues. You will never be able
to kill the soul of man even if you do kill the body. No wonder you don't know the soul of the new generation of Hebrews. You are amazed that those Hebrews whom you considered cowards, the Hebrews who were the slaughterers'

chosen victims for generations, have stood up against your tyranny, have fought against your armies and brought to naught all your schemes. You wonder why they go to the gallows with dignity and courage and with disdain for their torture. You can't understand how it has happened that those "Jew boys" forced you to seek refuge in your fortified ghettos and even there you don't find safety. You will never understand it. It will never occur to you that the new generation of Hebrews emerged out of two great processes: the soil of our homeland and the great disaster of our dispersion. The soil of our land put strength into our muscles, courage into our hearts and faith into our souls. Our land brought back to us the great tradition which was dormant in our people for so many generations: the tradition of the heroism of the Maccabees and Bar Kochba.

"The other influence is the unprecedented disaster of the dispersion. It taught us that we stand in a fight not only for our freedom, but for our very survival. It taught us that if we remain enslaved we shall all perish. It taught us that unless we take our fate into our own hands we shall go down in ignominy. It taught us that we have but one choice left, to fight or to vanish from God's earth. It removed from us any trace of fear or cowardice. Yes, British officers, before you stand men—not only here but in every corner of this country —men who know no fear, men who fear not even death. For how could death be fearsome to the sons of the people who lost millions in one great nightmare — millions who were slaughtered without rhyme or reason? When we remember our lost brethren, and we remember them always, our heart swells with happiness that it was given to us not to be trampled as they were, that it was given to us to fight for our country, to live in our homeland and to write a chapter of glorious heroism in the history of our people. We are proud that it was given to us to leave a legacy to generations yet unborn not of cowardice and slaughter, but of courage and revolt.

"You British tyrants will never understand the soul of free men walking to the gallows—as did Gruner and his comrades who went with a song in their hearts, a song of faith and hope. And this you will certainly not understand how I, a young Hebrew standing here before you and facing death, am giving thanks to the Lord that he made it my lot to suffer for my country and my people.

" 'Praised be the Lord, the Ruler of the Universe, who has kept me in life and has brought me to this day.' "

THE POLITICAL BATTLE

On June 16, the day when the UN Commission opened its first session in Jerusalem, the British officers, on orders from Ernest Bevin, pronounced the death "sentence" on three of the *Irgun soldiers*. The younger two, Amnon Michaelov and Nachman Zitterbaum, were "sentenced" to life imprisonment. Every person in the *Yishuv* understood that this "sentence" was intended as an answer to the UN and its Commission, which had requested all the parties concerned to make possible its work. All realized that the situation had been sharpened because Bevin had viewed the "sentence" as a matter of prestige. The *Irgun* was therefore very pessimistic concerning the general appeal of the *Yishuv* to the High Commissioner and to the Commanding Officer to commute the "sentence" and to grant a pardon. It therefore began feverish preparations for action that would force the British to change their position.

The UN Commission was unable to continue with its regular business after the flagrant insult it had received at the hands of Bevin. At the very first closed session of the Commission, Granados demanded that it protest against the "verdict." After a drawn out debate, the Commission adopted a compromise resolution. It sent the following communication to Trygvie Lie, General Secretary of the UN:

"The UN Commission expresses the concern of the majority of its members over the regrettable consequences liable to result from the carrying out of the three death sentences which the military court pronounced on June 16, and over the difficulties of fulfilling the responsibilities which the UN has imposed upon it."

When the Commission made its decision public, the British were fit to be tied. They had long forgotten that they were in office in Palestine only by grace of the League of Nations Mandate. They had long grown accustomed to viewing Palestine as a British colony over which they alone had the only say. This is why they were so upset when suddenly a "new" factor which spoke with authority intervened. Sir Gurney, General Secretary of the Mandatory Government, sent the Commission the following letter:

"I have been directed to inform you of the following: Our Government has learned from the newspapers that the UN Commission has decided to consult the UN regarding the death sentence. I must inform you that the death sentence has not as yet been confirmed by the Commander-in-Chief. It has therefore not as yet gone into effect and it means that the legal authorities have not finished their work. In such guarded matters it is necessary to refrain from open discussion concerning the trial. The Commission's resolution refers to June 16 as the date of its first session. We do not believe that you wish to infer that the court handed down its verdict on the same day without regard to legal procedure. It is obvious that such an inference is groundless."

The Commission realized that the letter was not only a typical hypocritical British communication but that it was a vulgar letter impertinently written. Relations between the Commission and the Mandatory Government became so strained that the *London Times* could no longer hide the fact and clearly wrote that Gurney's letter had been too sharp and that the relations would have to be improved.

From the Jewish political point of view these developments were favorable. The bad relations between the Commission and the British were a factor that caused Judge Sandstrom, chairman of the Commission, already in the early days of the Commission's stay in Palestine, to get in touch with the *Irgun* and ask for a meeting with Menachem Beigin. But the lives of three men were at stake. The *Irgun* therefore continued to look for a trump card which would force the British to reverse the "verdict."

In the meantime, Judge Sandstrom continued to press for a meeting with Beigin. It was a difficult task for the *Irgun* to meet with a person who was surrounded by British spies and whose every step was reported by the correspondents of the world's leading newspapers. But the *Irgun* realized the value of such a meeting in which the UN Commission could hear true Jewish demands regarding a greater and not a partitioned Palestine, regarding England's intrigues, etc. Through the meeting the *Irgun* hoped to disabuse the Commission of the impression that the entire Zionist world had given up historic Palestine.

IN THE INTERNATIONAL ARENA

The first request for the meeting came to the *Irgun* through the correspondent of the United Press who had long been in contact with one of the *Irgun* officers. At first it was understood that only the chairman, Judge Sandstrom, was to meet with Menachem Beigin. Later he requested, however, that the vice-secretary Mr. Hoo also be present during the conversations. Still later he requested that Dr. Ralph Bunche, secretary of the Commission, be there in order to "make notes . . ." This meant therefore an official hearing for the *Irgun* by the Commission.

Mr. Hoo, Vice Secretary of U.N. Secretariat and Special Delegate of Trygve Lie to the U.N. Commission, with the Irgun contact man, "Jacobi," prior to his meeting Mr. Beigin.

On the night of June 24, the meeting was held in an underground place, of which Sandstrom later said: *It was the securest spot in the whole of Palestine.*

Under the very noses of the British army and police who occupied Tel Aviv and under the noses of scores of detectives who spied upon the Underground and all its movements on the one hand and on the UN Commission members, on the other; and despite the searching eyes of the leading foreign correspondents who dogged the footsteps of the UN Commission members and especially of its chairman, Sandstrom, the *Irgun* liaison officers worked out a plan for bringing Sandstrom and his companions to the meeting. Unobserved, Sandstrom, Hoo and Bunche left their official UN motor car in a busy Tel Aviv street and at the signal of a liaison officer quickly entered a private machine which stood nearby. No one noticed that at the chauffeur's side there sat another man whose duty it was to bring the Commission members to Mr. Beigin. The machine began to move swiftly, followed by two more cars whose job it was to guard the high officials from any harm. . . .

After a half hour's ride through various streets, the machine suddenly stopped. The Commission members were requested to transfer to another car which awaited them. This time a young girl sat at the chauffeur's side and gave directions concerning the route and the streets which were to be traversed. Police and military patrols passed up and down the streets but none could imagine that the important gentlemen were being accompanied by a young girl to a meeting with the man for whom they had been looking for years and for whose head they were prepared to give thousands of dollars. . . . In this manner the automobile drew up to a designated house. The Commission members were guided by their girl campanion into the house where the Commander of the Irgun, Menachem Beigin and two of his officers awaited them. The conversation then began.

Mr. Beigin and his two colleagues sat at the head of the table with their backs to the window, facing Mr. Sandstrom, who was flanked by Mr. Hoo and Dr. Bunche. Mr. Sandstrom began the discussion with the statement that the essential condition for the talk was that nothing should be released on this meeting during the period of the Commission's stay in Palestine. Mr. Beigin readily agreed to this.

Mr. Beigin then stated that first of all he wished to thank the Commission for the action taken with regard to the sentences imposed on the three members of his organization by the so-called military court. He and his organization, he said, had no illusions as to the outcome, but they appreciated the action, the more so in view of the acceptance by the Commission of the interpretation of the UN Assembly's resolution put forward in the Irgun's letter, as obliging the British to refrain from the use or threat of force.

Mr. Sandstrom then inquired as to the aims of the *Irgun* organization and the position which Commander Beigin held in it, or rather the authority with which he could speak for it.

RECOUNTS IRGUN HISTORY

Mr. Beigin stated that *Irgun Zvai Leumi* meant "National Military Organization." It was organized some years ago. Its object was to bring about the liberation of the country from foreign yoke, the attainment of freedom for the Jewish people and the restoration of Jewish rule in Eretz Israel. Before the war, the *Irgun* had defended the Jewish people against the organized attacks of Arab groups which were instigated by the British rulers. It had also brought thousands of Jewish repatriates into the country in order to save them from an unbearable future in Europe.

With the outbreak of the war against Nazism, the *Irgun* realized that Hitler contemplated the destruction of the Jews. For some years, therefore, the organization undertook no offensive measures in the country because of the danger facing Palestine from the Nazi aggression. The organization was kept intact, however. Some members entered various allied armies; others continued in Underground organizational work.

In the latter part of 1943 and early part of 1944 it became obvious that all the sacrifices of the Jewish people on the battlefields would be in vain and that the Jews of Palestine would be left under oppressive rule with no opportunity to bring back those who would wish to return to their Homeland.

IRGUN AIMS PROCLAIMED

Consequently the *Irgun* issued its declaration of December 1943 to the effect that there would be no more interruptions in its fight for freedom. News had also come from Europe at the time, although still unconfirmed, that the mass slaughter of Jews in Europe had begun on an unprecedented scale. The *Irgun* then began operations which were aimed against the administration but refrained from harming the troop concentrations in the country, since it was vital not to endanger the fight against Hitler. The *Irgun* proclaimed its aim as that of Jewish rule in Palestine and stated that it would fight until that objective was achieved. Following this proclamation, the operations which the *Irgun* carried out varied in size and scope. This stage of activity lasted for nearly two years.

In the meantime the British occupation regime continued to keep the gates shut, even though fully aware of the annihilation of the Jews in Europe. The British continued to sabotage every effort in Europe to save the Jews. The *Irgun* therefore continued its struggle. The British tried to overcome this resistance with the aid of the organized Jewish groups, including the Jewish Agency. Some Jewish bodies handed over to the authorities Jews suspected of aiding the *Irgun*.

The British made use of the so-called Emergency Regulations which had been promulgated in 1936-37. In their effort to break the spirit of the Jewish people in Palestine, they arrested people whom they suspected of *Irgun* affiliations, and placed them in concentration camps. Two hundred and fifty-one suspected persons, had been deported to a concentration camp in Eritrea. He emphasized that these were all alleged suspects and that no charges had been brought against them.

At this point Mr. Beigin referred to the letter which the *Irgun* had sent to the Commission that same day requesting that the Commission call on the three *Irgun* members imprisoned by the authorities.

NO ILLUSIONS ABOUT LABOR PARTY

When the British Labor Party came to power, the *Irgun* did not share the illusions entertained in other quarters that the party would keep its promises and said as much in a public statement at the time. However, the *Irgun* was prepared to wait, to postpone operations and give the new Government a chance to live up to its word. When Bevin's intentions became clear the *Haganah* decided to raise the banner of armed resistance in Palestine. The *Haganah* was the largest of the three organized Underground bodies, the other two being the FFI (Fighters for the Freedom of Israel), known as the Stern Group, and the *Irgun*. In October 1945 these three groups reached an agreement to join hands in armed resistance. This agreement remained effective for ten months and this was a period of large-scale operations.

According to *Irgun* practice, if a British official was regarded as a criminal, he was to be tried in absentia, in view of the circumstances of Underground activity. When a verdict was reached the order was given to carry out the sentence.

In response to a question as to whether any action was ever taken against Jews, Mr. Beigin replied that Jewish informers for the British Secret police had been condemned on occasion.

Reverting to the previous discussion on the relations among the three resistance groups, Mr. Beigin stated that all of the combined tasks of the three organizations during the period of October 1945 to August 1946 were carried out under the name of the Jewish Resistance Movement.

HAGANAH BREAKS RANKS

After ten months of co-operative activity, the *Haganah* decided to discontinue the struggle. The *Irgun,* on the other hand, decided to continue in the same spirit and in fact was further convinced of the necessity of intensifying the struggle. For in Palestine there had been instituted an unprecedented oppressive rule and hundreds of thousands of Jews were languishing without hope in the *galut.* Mr. Beigin stated that a memorandum would be sent to the Commission by the *Irgun* which would set forth very clearly and in detail the objectives and demands of the organization.

With regard to the organization of the *Irgun,* Mr. Beigin explained that it was organized and governed by the common consent of its members. "We are leaders of the organization and will remain leaders as long as we carry out our mandate," he said.

Continuing his historical review, Mr. Beigin observed that the entire history of the Jewish armed organization had begun 27 years before with the *Haganah.* In the early stages, there were elections of officers by the nucleus of the organization with the approval of the membership. The *Irgun* sprang from the *Haganah* and followed the same method of leadership.

Mr. Beigin emphasized that no personal decisions were made in the *Irgun*. All decisions, were adopted collectively and were therefore, majority decisions. There was no dictatorship.

OUTLINES AIMS

In summing up the aims of the *Irgun*, Mr. Beigin stated, these could be expressed simply as follows:

1. The *Irgun* considers *Eretz Israel* as the land of the Jewish people.

2. *Eretz Israel* consists of both sides of the *Jordan*, including Transjordan. "Transjordan," Mr. Beigin said, "is an English term that is incorrect." In the original Hebrew both sides of the Jordan were, in effect, called "Transjordan." The early Hebrews, he said, first conquered what is today known as Transjordan and crossed into Palestine from east to west. The *Irgun*, he pointed out, considers the whole territory as Jewish territory and aims at the creation of a Jewish Republic under a democratic government.

3. Immediate repatriation of all Jews wishing to be repatriated to Palestine. The exact number of potential Hebrew repatriates is unknown but runs into the millions. A choice should be given to all Jews who wish to return to Palestine. Their return is prevented only by British illegal rule and by British armed force, which should be removed. A Jewish government would undertake the repatriation of Jews with international help.

4. We reject any statement made by the Labor Party as to the transfer of any Arabs from the country. There is enough room in Palestine for all, both Jews and Arabs.

5. Since Britain has decided to keep the country under her own control by force of arms, there is no other way to accomplish our aims than to meet force with force.

In response to a question concerning Arab immigration from other countries Mr. Beigin replied that the question of admitting Arab immigrats was a matter for the future Jewish government of the State to decide, just as every State decides its immigration policy. The *Irgun* had no preconceived prejudice against anybody who might apply for a visa to the Hebrew State.

UNRESTRICTED REPATRIATION

The first task of a Jewish government would be to bring back to the country all Jews wishing to be repatriated. Beigin emphasized that every Jew had a natural right to return to Palestine, and that the Jews had a *de jure* majority in the country. In fact, he said, the Hebrews now are only a *de facto* minority in Palestine because the British would not admit all those who wished to enter. Once that obstacle was removed, it would be only a matter of months before they were the *de facto* majority as well. In reply to a question concerning the technical and fiscal difficulties of transferring large numbers of Jews to Palestine, Beigin referred to the statement made by a United States General that he could evacuate Jews from the European camps in a matter of weeks. He referred to the mass Turkish-Greek exchange of populations in 1922, effected in a matter of months. How much more was possible now, with the great advance in modern technical knowledge.

A PROVISIONAL GOVERNMENT

Mr. Beigin explained that the *Irgun* proposal was not to establish immediately a permanent Jewish government in Palestine but rather a provisional one to which power would be transferred for the specific task of accomplishing the repatriation of all Jews who wished to be repatriated. After this was accomplished, the provisional government would resign and then free elections would be held, with Jew and Arab participation. A permanent government would then be established. In this government there could be Arab ministers, perhaps an Arab Vice-President. The provisional government would be democratic because it would represent the rightful owners of the country. Beigin pointed out that this had happened in various countries, once in France and twice in Czechoslovakia.

The question was asked as to how long the provisional status would last. Mr. Beigin replied that it would last until all the rightful citizens of Palestine were in the country. But, he cautioned, one must understand that in the creation of the Jewish state and the repatriation of the Jews one cannot judge by normal circumstances and criteria. The Jews in Europe, he said, have gone through such an ordeal that they are prepared to live in tents in Palestine, if necessary. They will suffer when they come here and it will take time, but it can be done quickly.

AGAINST PARTITION

Mr. Sandstom asked whether the *Irgun* would dissolve when the state was created. Mr. Beigin replied: "Yes." When asked what the *Irgun* would do in the case of partition, he pointed out that none of the *Irgun* members would accept the carving up of any territory they considered the property of the Jewish State of Palestine, but it was too early to speak of what the methods of resistance to such steps would be.

Beigin was asked regarding the *Irgun* position if Jewish immigration were not to proceed as quickly as expected and the Arabs, continuing in the majority, should vote against immigration. He replied: "How could such elections take place in Palestine?" Such elections would be illegal because they would exclude all the Jews in exile who had a right to be in the country. Any Jew wishing to return to the country from which his ancestors were expelled had the right to do so.

ABSORPTIVE CAPACITY EXPLAINED

With regard to the absorptive capacity of the country Mr. Beigin pointed out that in ancient times there were between five and seven million people in Palestine. Transjordan, he said, is absolutely empty, with only four people to each square kilometer.

When asked how the Hebrews would solve the problem of over-population that would arise say 300 years later even if they developed their state on both sides of the Jordan, his reply was: "What will they do in 300 years in other countries, like China?"

It was pointed out to Mr. Beigin that the settlement of Jews in Palestine was a cause of Arab resentment and that this might lead to forceful opposition. He was asked what the *Irgun* would do in such a contingency. He replied that the *Irgun* did not give credence to any independent Arab opposition. All Arab opposition, he said, was instigated by the British themselves. True, theoretically the Arabs were opposed to any increase in the Jewish population. He cited a recent article in a Cairo newspaper which had quoted Jamal Husseini to the effect that particion, too, would mean war. But, questioned Mr. Beigin, are such threats to be taken seriously? If war is inevitable in any event, why sacrifice Jewish rights? On the other hand, if these were empty threats, as he believed them to be, then they should be disregarded.

DISCLAIMS HEBREW-ARAB CONFLICT

The *Irgun,* Mr. Beigin said, would defend the Jewish people against any attackers, Arab or otherwise. But he did not belive that the Arabs would actually go to war. This, he said, is all British propaganda. If the British left the country, he continued, there would be peace.

Mr. Beigin suggested that the Commission inquire of Mr. Gurney, Chief Secretary of the Palestine Government, as to when the so-called Arab High Committee was elected by the Arab people.

Mr. Sandstrom asked Beigin what proof he might adduce for his allegation that Arab opposition had been instigated by the British. He replied that after the Balfour Declaration British generals had made public speeches stating there would be no Jewish state in Palestine and that only limited immigration would be permitted. Unofficially, he added, high British officials would visit Arab villages to spread rumors of impending Jewish attacks and encourage the Arabs to oppose the Hebrews. He said that the *Haganah* had in its archives detailed proof of these allegations. Mr. Beigin pointed out that despite Haj Amin El Husseini's instigation of the Arabs against the Jews in Jerusalem in 1920, he had been granted a pardon and undemocratically given the post of Mufti.

THE FALSIFIED CENSUS

Mr. Beigin was asked again regarding his reaction to a proposal for partition. He replied that the *Irgun* had rejected partition and would fight against it, first of all, as a matter of principle. A country, he said, is something no one is entitled to trifle with. We cannot give up any part of our country, which has been defended for generations by Jews who hoped to return to it. Thus, he said, we reject partition on the basis of principle. Partition, moreover is impractical. Allegations have been made at United Nations meetings that Hebrews and Arabs cannot live together, that their aims and aspirations are irreconcilable, and that therefore partition was necessary. But actually if these allegations are true then partition is impossible, since no line of demarcation can actually be drawn to provide that the peoples of this country live apart from each other. We have no confidence in government statistics, he said, which are fabricated for political purposes. For example, the British Government has said that there were 1,200,000 Arabs in Palestine. But where are they to be found? A census was taken in 1931 and the Arab village chiefs received a shilling for each birth they reported.

The nucleus of large populations is always to be found in cities. Where, Mr. Beigin asked, were large Arab cities? The only Arab cities worthy of the name were Jaffa, Nablus and parts of Haifa and Jerusalem. The *Irgun* proposes that a census of the whole of Palestine be carried out under international control. Mr. Beigin continued to explain that if the large plan of partition were adopted (that is, along the lines of the Jewish Agency proposal), there would be an Arab majority, according to present government statistics. In order to establish the Hebrew majority there, repatriation would be needed, just as it would be required for the country as a whole.

AGAINST POPULATION TRANSFER

Mr. Beigin stated that the *Irgun* was opposed to the transfer of population, either Arab or Jewish, which some people had suggested as a means of carrying out partition. It is unethical, he maintained, to uproot people from their homes against their will. There was no need, in fact, for any transfer of population from Palestine or within Palestine, since there was room for all here. There is no possibility, he said, of exchanging populations. Under a partition scheme, the majority of the Hebrews now in Palestine would live in a ghetto state behind an artificial boundary. No exchange of population in Palestine could be made without use of force.

Mr. Beigin was asked whether the *Irgun* would accept a solution which would provide for a federated state in Palestine and an over-all government, with the different parts having self-government somewhat along the lines of the states in the United States or the cantons in Switzerland. He replied that the form of government in the future state of Palestine and the details of its constitution, should be approved by the parliament of Palestine. It was first necessary to decide on the principle. What is Palestine from the viewpoint of history? Is it a Jewish state or not? A federated state along the lines of the Morrison plan, he said, was what the British were trying to get the United Nations to adopt in order to perpetuate their illegal occupation rule.

PALESTINE IS JEWISH TERRITORY

Mr. Beigin stated that the *Irgun* did not base its claim on the League of Nations Mandate but on the historical fact that

Palestine had been Jewish territory for generations. Already 3,000 years ago there was a Jewish state here, from which the ancestors of the present-day Jews were forcibly expelled by the Romans. The people of Lidice, whose town had been obliterated by the Germans, came back after the war to rebuild their homes and lives. So it is with the Jewish return to Palestine.

The Arabs, on the other hand, had never created an Arab government in Palestine. This was never an Arab country. Mr. Beigin said that the *Irgun* reply to any proposal depended on the condition that the Jewish people be allowed freely to return to Palestine under their rule and on the principle of the unity of the whole country. If this was granted all the rest would be a mere detail. A Jewish government was a prerequisite to the repatriation of the Jews. Under a federated system the door might be closed to repatriation in some parts of the country and this would oppose one of the *Irgun's* basic principles.

FOR AGARIAN REFORMS

Mr. Beigin was asked what might happen to Arab land holdings in a Jewish State. He replied that land now held by Arabs would be retained by them, but that in the new Palestine there would be need for agarian reforms. There are vast lands held by Arab feudal landlords which have never been cultivated, and large tracts are held by the British. The government of the new Palestine would have to adjust this situation.

Mr. Standstrom inquired whether the *Irgun* would fight against a solution which might be acceptable to the majority of the Jewish people but which did not meet all the aims and conditions of the *Irgun* itself. Mr. Beigin replied that no majority of this generation of the Jewish people had the right to relinquish the historic title of the Jewish people to their country, which belonged to all generations to come as well.

Mr. Beigin was asked if he would state the reasons for the extreme methods of the opposition to the British—was it to force the evacuation of their troops, to release Jewish prisoners, or to achieve any other purpose? He replied that we desired the complete evacuation of the British rule, the setting up of a provisional government and the creation of the Jewish State.

PEOPLE SUPPORT IRGUN

In response to a suggestion that the *Irgun* lacked popular backing, Beigin asked: 'Do you really believe we do not have the support of the Jewish people? If this were true, how could we resist in the face of the great number of British police and troops here? We are convinced that we must fight or the Jewish people will be destroyed. We are not professional fighters. We don't take pleasure in shooting or being shot. Remember we have lost six million people and every Jewish life is all the more precious to us. But we fight for a purpose, to prevent subjugation and utter destruction.'

Mr. Beigin pointed out that while his organization's struggle had created difficulties for the Jewish people—curfews, restrictions, retaliations, etc., — suffering, as every people that had fought knew, was inseparable from the struggle for independence. There was no doubt that the overwhelming majority of the Jewish people were in favor of the struggle.

Raising a legal point, Mr. Beigin contended that even under the Mandate there was absolutely no justification for a British

Military Court in Palestine. The *Irgun* members considered themselves bona fide fighters engaged in a justified fight and they viewed the British as illegal occupants. He stated that the *Irgun* had had many casualities and wounded as a result of its operations. The British, he said, executed four *Irgun* soldiers, yet the *Irgun* did not cease its activities but rather intensified them. It inflicted heavy losses on the enemy and the price is not yet paid. After the executions, he observed, came the storming of Acre which was no small feat. The fight will go on. The British suggestion that they might cease executing *Irgun* members if the *Irgun* stopped fighting was ridiculous blackmail. "Go to Acre, and ask the three boys 'sentenced' to death whether they are prepared to buy their lives at the price of our struggle. They sent me letters, just as Dov Gruner did, saying: 'Whatever happens, fight on. We are all prepared to give our lives.'" No member of the *Irgun,* he said, had ever asked for mercy or a pardon from the occupation regime.

FURTHER COMMISSIONS FEARED

Mr. Beigin expressed the fear that the General Assembly would not have enough time in September to deal with the problem and that a second commission would be appointed to come to Palestine again and that during all this time men, women and children would be languishing in concentration camps in Europe. He explained that the Stern Group was a splinter group of the *Irgun.* They too are fighters, he observed. The Stern Group became an independent group in 1940 for various reasons. It was widely believed, he said, that the reason for the split was that Abraham Stern, then a member of the *Irgun* High Command, had opposed the *Irgun* proclamation of an armistice with the British during the war against Hitler. This was not true. Stern had subscribed to that proclamation together with the rest of the High Command. The split had come a year later. The relations between the two groups were now good. The *Irgun* was larger but he would not say that it was better.

Mr. Beigin then asked if there was any possibility that the Commission might honor the request of the *Irgun* to call some members imprisoned at Acre as witnesses. Mr. Sandstrom replied frankly: "There is very little possibility. We have done just about all we can do. We wonder why should these three men be best able to give evidence of terror in the camps." In answer to the latter point Mr. Beigin pointed out that these men had been before the Military Court, had themselves experienced maltreatment and had witnessed it in the case of others.

Mr. Standstrom then observed that there were undoubtedly other witnesses who could testify similarly. Mr. Beigin replied that the case of these three was a special one. They could tell of men who were shot and wounded after their capture in the Acre prison break, of wounded who were shot dead while lying in agony on the ground, of others who died because they were given no medical treatment or even water.

Mr. Beigin stated that he was not sure that the intervention of the Commission would yield any result. In any case, any such intervention could be couched in diplomatic terms, as was the resolution of the Commission concerning the "sentence" of these *Irgun* men. He added that to his mind a precedent for granting the *Irgun* request could be found in the Greek investigation by the UN Security Council.

IRGUN KEEPS WORD

At the close of the discussion, the Chairman mentioned the agreement which had been reached at its beginning that there would be no publicity about this meeting. Mr. Beigin replied that the *"Irgun* always keeps its word. Ask the British. They will tell you." He agreed that at some later date, when the Commission had left Palestine, the Chairman, if he saw fit, could release the story of the meeting and the notes of the discussion, provided he would be given a prior opportunity to review the material before its release. This was agreed to by Mr. Sandstrom.

'SENTENCE' UPHELD

Because of his concern with "prestige," Bevin hastened the crisis. Only a few hours after the conversation of the Chairman of the UN Commission with Menachem Beigin, the newspapers reported that the new Commander-in-Chief of the British Army, General MacMillan, had confirmed the "sentence" and had warned his soldiers and officers against leaving camps unarmed and if they did have to do so it was to be only on official business and in groups. The *Haganah* also mobilized its strength for preventing the *Irgun* from arresting any Englishmen. For over two weeks it seemed that the three *Irgun* men would go to the gallows and that the British would not only go unpunished but would get from the Jews themselves a free hand to hang and shoot whomsoever they wished. But the *Irgun* had not given up hope. While continuing its efforts to arrest British soldiers, who now seldom showed themselves, they began to dig a tunnel in the neighborhood of "Bet Hadar" in Tel Aviv, where the British were strongly entrenched. The tunnel was to lead into the "Bet Hadar" building, the center of the British stronghold.

IRGUN ARRESTS

After many attempts, the *Irgun* finally succeeded on Friday, June 12, in arresting two British sergeants, Marvin Face and Edward Martin. Both were employed in the Intelligence Service and had spied on the Jews. They were arrested in the vicinity of Nathanya. News of the arrest travelled like lightning around the world. Both the British and the *Haganah* quickly mobilized thousands of men in order to search for the sergeants. Immediately following the arrests, Nathanya was isolated but none of the searches yielded any results.

On June 14, Brigadier Moore proclaimed a state of martial law in Nathanya. The British and the *Haganah* were certain that the *Irgun* had been unable to remove the sergeants from the town and decided to search every house and examine every foot of earth. . . . Bevin's international "prestige" dictated the hanging of the three Jews. Bevin knew that the sergeants would also pay with their lives and his forces in Palestine wanted to do everything possible to save them. The entire population was shut in and any attempt to open a window or door endangered life. The army robbed anything it liked and showed great brutality to the people.

The British were unable to maintain their barbaric martial law for long. The members of the UN Commission, Granados and Fabrigat, hearing of the events in Nathanya, visited the place in the company of foreign correspondents, particularly those

from America. The British were unable to keep them out. Upon
its return to Jerusalem, the party prepared to make public the
scandalous story of British barbarism. The British began to
hem and haw and tried to explain that martial law was justified
because . . . they had found 15 *Irgun* leaders among whom were
two men they had long been seeking. The foreign correspondents
laughed at this "defense." The truth was self-evident. The
British were forced to remove the "curfew" during the day so
that supplies could be brought to Nathanya, and retained it only
at night on the roads. The inhabitants, however, were unable
to leave the city and the searches were continued.

The *Haganah,* too, did not rest. It spread its network of
espionage. The spies succeeded in finding traces of the tunnel
which the *Irgun* had dug under "Bet Hadar" in Tel Aviv. When
the *Irgun* discovered this fact, it stopped all work and left a
sign at the place saying: *"The tunnel is mined."* Because of
gross negligence, the *Haganah* men who were to remove the
mines were blown up. The British naturally triumphed in their
"victory." But the *Haganah* received two insults at the hands
of the British for their efforts: 1) In Parliament a member suggested that the families of the *Haganah* men receive aid from
the British treasury. . . . 2) On July 18, the same day on which
the *Haganah* discovered the tunnel, British soldiers who were
searching through the neighborhood found and confiscated a
large cache of *Haganah* arms. In the *Haganah* ranks there was
much sharp discussion. Many of the members demanded that
co-operation with the British be stopped. The debates were so
heated that a "compromise" had to be adopted . . . the *Haganah*
would fight the *Irgun* on its own. . . .

The British well understood the "difference" between the
"two" approaches. When the British information officer, Colonel

British police gaze in amazement at entrance to tunnel through which Irgun planned to blast army headquarters in Citrus House.

Sheffield, was asked at a press conference whether the *Haganah* was still co-operating with the army, he replied: "Don't call it by that name, it isn't popular with the Jews."

On Tisha B'Av, July 27, two weeks after the proclamation of martial law in Nathanya, the British were forced to revoke it and admit that it had failed. They had neither found the sergeants nor arrested any important *Irgun* men. There was general rejoicing over the revoking of martial law but that same evening the Jerusalem radio announced that the "sentence" against the three *Irgun* men would be carried out that night. This time the British had openly and in advance declared their intention of going through with the hangings. They invited

Curfew in Nathanya.

Rabbi Uchna to come from Haifa to Acre in order to say the *viddui* with the three men. They did not proclaim any "curfew."

THEIR LAST NIGHT

The *Irgun,* however, well understood the British trick. The British intentionally did everything in the open but in the greatest of secrecy they mobilized strong military forces throughout the country and particularly in the neighborhood of Nathanya. The *Haganah* also mobilized all its strength against the *Irgun.* Both believed that when the *Irgun* learned that its men were hanged that night, it would retaliate against the British sergeants. Any "curfew" which the British might have proclaimed would have hampered the *Haganah* in its searches.

The trick, however, was unsuccessful and the British reckoned without their host. With gnashing of teeth, *Irgun* men

accompanied the families of their faithful soldier heroes who
were being brought by the police to Safed for the funeral. With
gnashing of teeth they brought Weiss' only sister (no one knew
as yet that a brother of Weiss had escaped at the beginning of
the Nazi invasion of Czechoslovakia and that he was the
captain of an air squadron in London—he is today in the Israel
Army) from Ramat Gan to Tel Aviv in order that she be able
to attend her brother's funeral. With gnashing of teeth and
bloodshot eyes they accompanied Rabbi Uchna from Haifa on
his trip to Acre to say the *viddui* with their friends. But none
lost patience or control.

That night the Jewish arrestees in Acre strained to hear any
sound that might issue from the death cell. At 3 A.M. they
heard the singing of the *Hatikvah*. In that dark corridor which
led from the death cell to the gallows Avshalom Habib walked
for the last time and sang *Od Lo Avdah Tikvatenu,* 'Our hope
is not yet lost." An hour later Yaakov Weiss walked down
the corridor with the same song and at 5 A.M. went the last
of the three, Meir Nakar. The Jewish arrestees took up the
song and accompanied them until the British hangman drew the
noose around the necks of the condemned. They continued to
sing without them and for them, "Our hope is not yet lost." It
was the night of the Tisha B'Av fast, of July 28, 1947.

HANGING OF THE SERGEANTS

By carrying out the death "sentence" against the three *Irgun*
soldiers, Bevin had condemned the two sergeants to death.
This the British also realized. They made a last effort to find

the two sergeants but themselves no longer believed they would succeed. The official Jewish bodies "saw" it differently. Even before the corpses of the three heroes had cooled, demands were voiced by all the official authorities that the *Irgun* immediatel: free the sergeants. With cowardice and fear they themselvess indicated to the British what to do. . . . *"There will be pogroms, we will be slaughtered in the streets . . .,"* was their cry. A few hours after the threefold murder at Acre, I met with the Mayors of Tel Aviv, Petach Tikvah and others. I tried to make them understand that the British had already tried everything and failed and that the *Irgun* would reply to pogroms with pogroms against every British soldier who would show himself in a Jewish neighborhood. But fear is unreasonable, and their fear was great, exceedingly great.

On July 31, the *Irgun* announced officially that the two sergeants had been hanged. It added the warning that the site of their hanging was mined and that the men, British or Jewish, who would remove their bodies should be careful. Twenty-four hours passed before the British and the *Haganah* found the place—a thicket two kilometers from Nathanya.

SMOKE BUT NO FIRE

The next few days were tense ones. The British kept quiet but it was their silence that perturbed the *Yishuv*. There were no epithets left for the official Jewish bodies to throw at the *Irgun*. There were no appeals left that they had not addressed to the British. But still the British kept quiet. The secret of their silence was quite simple: they were too confused and what's more—they were broken.

This was the first time in British colonial history that "natives' dared to inflict harm on the "sacred" bodies of British soldiers. In the British press there appeared letters of protest against the Palestine officials who had obstinately refused to pardon the three "terrorists." Bevin particularly was attacked and it was pointed out that when the lives of the British officers, who were held as hostages for Ashbel and Simchon, were at stake he did grant a pardon but when it came to sergeants he threw away their lives because of his prestige.

British prestige collapsed on all fronts, and particularly on the political front. The UN Commission on Palestine which was at that time holding sessions in Switzerland and witnessing the events in Palestine, came to a definite conclusion that Great Britain could no longer govern the country. Even members of the Commission whose governments instructed them to take a pro-British stand, had realized that if a force of a hundred thousand British soldiers could not cope with the situation there was nothing left for Britain to do but quit.

Also in the United States, where foreign policy on the United Nations level tended generally to run parallel with British foreign policy, nothing could be done when the report of the Commission came up for discussion at the General Assembly save to back the conclusions contained in the report. Among all the other reasons which determined the United States' attitude towards the Palestine question in the discussion of November 1947, this chapter of the Palestine armed conflict that started with the breaching of the Acre fortress and finished with the hanging of the two sergeants, played an important if not the most important part.

Bevin realized that he lost the Palestine battle not only in the political field, but also in the military field. The British Military Commander for Palestine and Trans-Jordan found it impossible to send any more Hebrew fighters to the gallows. Three days after the hanging of the two sergeants, five of the "Fighters for Freedom of Israel" (Stern Group) faced "trial." They were captured while putting up armed resistance and shot at the British troops. In spite of this the British Military Commander saw the futility of ordering his "judges" to proclaim a death sentence. Capital punishment had received a deadly blow in Palestine and was gone for good from the country.

Also in the field of British administration came the reign of chaos. British threats of imposing Martial Law upon the Jewish community and of drowning the fighting underground in its blood, were not taken seriously. A few days after the hanging of the sergeants, the British administration was still at a loss as to what action should be taken. British soldiers in Palestine and their families in England had put up a hue and cry not to get them involved in the vicious circle of blood. A few British soldiers tried to get rough, but were soon surpressed by Underground action, which kept them confined to camps. As some gesture of saving face was expected, the British administration fell back on the old game of haphazard arrests.

In the night hours of August 5th, 1947, were arrested 37 Revisionist and Betar leaders. Also interned were Mr. Israel Rokach, Mayor of Tel Aviv, Mr. Avraham Krinitzi, Mayor of Ramat-Gan and Mr. Ben-Ami, Mayor of Nathanya. Brit Trumpledor (Betar) was declared an illegal organization. This was the reaction. This was the agonized convulsion of a regime that collapsed like a house of cards. British Military Headquarters were unable to control the scared troops, who pleaded for their immediate release. The police headquarters could not control its force which was caught like a leaf in the storm. The staff of the British administration took refuge behind the barbed-wire with which they had encircled themselves.

The breach made in the Acre fortress had a deep and shattering effect on the Mandatory power. The hanging of the two

A group of prominent Jewish leaders imprisoned in Latrun concentration camp. They were known as "V.I.P.," very important prisoners. Abraham Krinitzi and Itzhak Gurion are third and fourth from right.

sergeants had irreparably broken British prestige in Palestine And, when Mr. Bevin appeared before the UN General Assembly in the months of October-November 1947, he could not master one-third of the votes to support his schemes for remaining in Palestine. He knew then that the Underground had defeated him, and indeed, he evacuated Palestine three to four months before the time limit set by the UN.

Menachem Beigin, disguised as Rabbi
Sussover during underground period.

Salute to the Heroic Dead*

By Menachem Beigin

W E have come to you from all corners of the land and
stand before you with trepidation, resignation and holi-
ness. We are here to inform you that the wicked arm
which plucked you from amongst us is broken and that the
British oppressive rule has been removed from our homeland.
The hangmen who led you to the gallows have been driven out.
The land has been rid of the British army of occupation. The
basis has been laid for Jewish independence in the land. The
State of Israel has risen and tens of thousands of Jewish soldiers

---

* The first anniversary of the death of the martyrs Avshalom
Habib, Meir Nakar and Yaakov Weiss (August 1948) occurred a
few months after the declaration of Jewish independence. Mr.
Menachem Beigin, the commander of the *Irgun Zvai Leumi* during the rebellion against the British occupying forces, emerged
from years of underground activity into the open. Together with
hundreds of *Irgun* soldiers he took part in a pilgrimage to the
graves of the martyrs in Safed and delivered the following address. Mr. Beigin has kindly granted permission to use this address
as an epilogue to the book.   *The Author.*

A pilgramage to the cemetery at Safed where
hanged Irgun heroes lie buried.

stand ready to beat back the enemy, destroy the foe and realize
the national hope of independence for the entire homeland.

Valiant soldiers—gather today from Jerusalem, the Eternal
City, from Negba, from the north, from tumultous Tel Aviv,
from Nathanya, from Haifa, the city of the future, and from all
sections of the homeland; valiant soldiers—your brothers in
arms and battle, stormers of the Acre prison, and liberated Acre
prisoners whom you freed and protected with your bodies and
for whom you gave souls in purity—all of us have come here
today to bring you tidings of your victory. Your work has
been rewarded! Your sacrifice has not been in vain! Your
blood has not been spilled for nought! You have not laid down
your young lives needlessly. You have been victorious, for the
cruel enemy who snapped your necks on the gallows and who
wished to break our people was himself stopped by you and
your fighting brethren.

Your brethren from all ends of the land report to you that your dream has been realized! A Jewish army and a Jewish government is now ours! There is hope in our generation for the liberation of the entire homeland. . . . No longer do we stand alone in the front of battle, nor is it only our fighting sons who have taken up the struggle; the entire people carries high the flag of freedom—the same flag which you raised in the open and also in the Underground, in the death cell and also on the gallows. It is the same flag which you refused to relinquish until the last gasp of your holy, pure breath.

You are not alone, our holy and pure brethren who shine as the brightness of the firmament, you are not alone in these mountains of Galilee. You decreed the fate of the oppressor's rule by storming the Bastille. At your side lie the four who went to the

Menachem Beigin, former Commander-in-Chief of the Irgun Zvai Leumi, presently head of Cherut Delegation in the Knesset.

Menachem Beigin, flanked by Irgun officers, standing at graves of hanged Irgunists.

gallows with a song of faith and freedom, and not far from here lies your brother—the first of our national martyrs, the first who sang and fulfilled the command *Lamut o lichbosh et Ha-har* (to "die or take the mountain"). Not far from here rest the fallen stormers of Acre and those who died before they could be liberated; and nearby lie the heroes of Galilee who fell in the recent war and those of olden times. None of them gave up until the last drop of blood.

And you converse amongst yourselves during the night, you who died heroes' deaths in our time and the ten martyrs of old— you who have fallen in Galilee in our time and you who died of old. There is conversation among you, the greatest conversation of its kind ever heard in the world. A golden chain links you all. At night your souls commune with one another concerning Galilee and the entire land, concerning our eternal people which has been beset by so many enemies and has been able to withstand them because it never forsook its faith. It is not the voice of lamentation and bitter weeping which is heard when you speak to each other, but joy breaks forth from the heavens above and gladness and delight are heard in the world. By virtue of

this faith there arose heroes whose like has not been seen among
our people since the days of *Rabbi Akiba* and *Bar Kochba.* By
virtue of this faith we renewed the ancient days of our land.

From the depths of Jewish sorrow and anguish there arose
those who stormed the enemy's fortresses and beat him back,
those who went to the gallows singing a song to the very end.
It is therefore no longer the voice of lamentation and bitter weeping which is heard but rather that of joy, gladness and delight,
both from your own holy and pure souls and those of our
fathers.

For we neither shamed our fathers nor forsook their way when
we embarked on our march toward freedom. And if many fell
by the way, others have taken their places and carry high the
flag of the war of liberation, so that we are able to report to
you that the vision for which you have fallen and sanctified the
name of God has been fully realized.

For the entire land on both sides of the *Jordan* is ours. It was
and will be ours and our people will dwell in it for ever.

Ye mountains of Galilee that have received the bodies of the
heroic dead of Israel for seventy generations, let there be dew
and rain upon you! We have liberated you forever. Because
of this sacred blood the crown of *Hermon* will be *ours.*

Members and soldiers of *Irgun Zvai Leumi*: attention!

At the graves of our national martyrs let us all take the oath to
Jerusalem which as yet has not been fully liberated and to
whose liberation they dedicated their lives and their death.

"If I forget thee, O Jerusalem, let my right hand forget its
cunning. Let my tongue cleave to the roof of my mouth, if I
remember thee not; if I set not Jerusalem above my chiefest
joy."

1. Zeev (Vladimir) Jabotinsky, who inspired the Jewish revolt. 2. David Raziel, who launched the war for Israel's liberation. 3. Menachem Beigin, under whose leadership the Irgun freed Palestine from the British yoke. 4. Shlomo Ben Yosef, the first Jewish patriot to be hanged by the British. 5. Dov Gruner. 6. Eliezer Kashani. 7. Eliahu Hakim. 8. Eliahu Bet Tzuri. 9. Yachiel Dresner (Dov Rosenbaum). 10. Mordecai Alkashi. 11. Moshe Barazani and Meir Feinstein (12) who took their own lives to escape the British gallows. 13. Meir Nakar. 14. Yaakov Weiss. 15. Avshalon Habib.

(Rights to this illustration are reserved by Tnuat Hacherut in Israel)

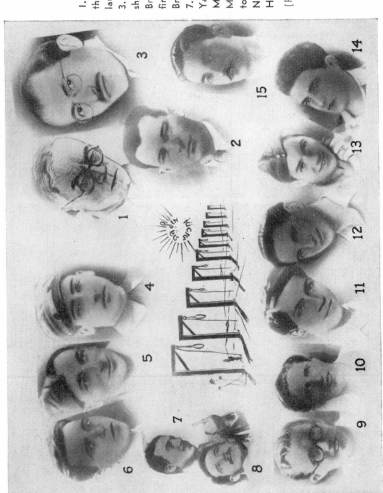